Advance Praise for *Kids & Sports*

"*Kids & Sports* is a wonderful, practical book for parents that covers the entire spectrum—from infancy to adolescence, from prevention to when to seek treatment, from the healthy athlete to the athlete with a chronic illness, from kids who just play sports for fun to star athletes. *Kids & Sports* is so accessible, it is great for kids to read, too."

—*Angela Diaz, M.D.,*
Chair, Division of Adolescent Medicine, Mount Sinai Hospital

"Dr. Eric Small provides all the answers that every sports parent could ever have about their child's involvement in youth athletics. "

—*Rick Wolff, chairman, The Center for Sports Parenting*

"As we try to motivate our ever-more-sedentary youth population towards activity, Dr. Small's book arms us with tips and techniques to get kids moving, safely and successfully." —*Marsha Johnson Evans, Ph.D.,*
National Executive Director, Girl Scouts of the USA

"This useful book addresses thorny issues, such as when to permit a child to specialize in a sport, when is weight-training appropriate, and how to encourage and support the obese and non-athletic child."

— *Jeffrey Gershel, M.D., Chief of Service,*
Department of Pediatrics, Jacobi Medical Center

"Eric Small does a superb job of answering the questions every parent should ask about kids and sports. His expertise shines through and his easy-to-read style reduces even the toughest to pronounce medical conditions to understandable prose. This is one book every parent can find useful." —*Don Yaeger, Associate Editor,* Sports Illustrated

"Dr. Small hits the nail on the head when he states that children are not miniature adults. A must read for all of us who in some way are involved in youth sports." —*E. Paul Roetert, Ph.D., Director of Administration,*
USA Tennis High Performance Program

"Dr. Small has done an excellent job of covering a wide variety of topics in a way that is both readable and practical."

—*Mimi Johnson, M.D., Pediatric and Young Adult Sports Medicine Specialist*

"I recommend this book for every mother and father of an athlete whether the athlete competes at the highest level or just in the neighborhood pick-up games." —*Dempsey Springfield, M.D.,*
Chair, Leni & Peter W. May Department of Orthopaedics,
Mount Sinai School of Medicine

"Dr. Small has presented a comprehensive topic in simple informative language that players, parents, and coaches can relate to in a direct, positive fashion. By using the book, young athletes and their parents can expect short- and long-term results." —*David Glackin, United States*
Professional Tennis Association teacher

"A must-read for anyone involved with youth sports. This in-depth reference guide is informative and should be included on every athletic director's bookshelf." —*David McGuckin, Director of Athletics,*
Mamaroneck High School

"A must-have resource that allows parents to guide their young athletes towards success in their sports, as well as through life. By offering specific methods and timetables, Eric Small takes the guess-work out of the process." —*Wendy Mlinar, United States Figure Skating*
Association (USFSA) Skating and Dance Judge

"I believe this book belongs on the bookshelf of every parent, teacher, and coach interested in the physical and emotional development of children through sports." —*Kristjan T. Ragnarsson, M.D.,*
Chairman and Dr. Lucy G. Moses Professor,
Department of Rehabilitation Medicine, Mount Sinai Hospital

"*Kids & Sports* is a one-of-a-kind resource that all parents and coaches would benefit from having. Dr. Small has created a comprehensive guide for providing children with an enjoyable and healthy sports experience." —*David Goodman, Executive Director, Philadelphia Youth Tennis, Inc.,*
and owner/operator of the Arthur Ashe Youth Tennis Center
and National Junior Tennis League of Philadelphia

KIDS & SPORTS

**Everything You and Your Child Need to Know
About Sports, Physical Activity, and Good Health—
A Doctor's Guide for Parents and Coaches**

Eric Small, M.D., F.A.A.P.
with Linda Spear

NEWMARKET PRESS

This book is published in the United States of America.

This book is designed to provide accurate and authoritative information in regard to the subject matter covered. It is not intended as a substitute for medical advice from a qualified physician. The reader should consult his or her medical, health, or other competent professional before adopting any of the suggestions in this book or drawing inferences from it.

The author and publisher specifically disclaim all responsibility for any liability, loss, or risk, personal or otherwise, that is incurred as a consequence, directly or indirectly, of the use and application of any of the contents of this book.

First Edition

10   9   8   7   6   5   4   3   2   1
ISBN 1-55704-532-1 (paperback)

10   9   8   7   6   5   4   3   2   1
ISBN 1-55704-498-8 (hardcover)

Library of Congress Cataloging-in-Publication Data
Small, Eric.
Kids & sports : everything you and your child need to know about sports, physical activity, and good health : a doctor's guide for parents and coaches.—1st ed.
p. cm.
Includes bibliographical references and index.
ISBN 1-55704-498-8 (hard : alk. paper)
1. Sports for children—Handbooks, manuals, etc. 2. Sports for children—Physiological aspects. I. Title: Kids and sports. II. Title.
GV709.2 .S52 2002
613.7'042—dc21   2001051199

QUANTITY PURCHASES
Companies, professional groups, clubs, and other organizations may qualify for special terms when ordering quantities of this title. For information, write Special Sales Department, Newmarket Press, 18 East 48th Street, New York, NY 10017; call (212) 832-3575; fax (212) 832-3629; or e-mail mailbox@newmarketpress.com.

Design by Betty Lew
All illustrations by Simon Sullivan
Manufactured in the United States of America.

OTHER NEWMARKET PARENTING GUIDES INCLUDE:

Beyond the Big Talk: Every Parent's Guide to Raising Sexually Healthy Children, by Debra W. Haffner, M.P.H.
From Diapers to Dating: A Parent's Guide to Raising Sexually Healthy Children, by Debra W. Haffner, M.P.H.
How to Help Your Child Overcome Your Divorce, by Elissa P. Benedek, M.D., and Catherine F. Brown, M.Ed.
In Time and With Love, by Marilyn Segal, Ph.D.
Keep Your Kids Tobacco-Free, by Robert Schwebel, Ph.D.
Mommy, My Head Hurts: A Doctor's Guide to Your Child's Headaches, by Sarah Cheyette, M.D.

My Body My Self Books, by Lynda Madaras & Area Madaras
My Feelings, My Self, by Lynda Madaras & Area Madaras
Saying No Is Not Enough, Rev. Ed., by Robert Schwebel, Ph.D.
The "What's Happening to My Body?" Books, by Lynda Madaras & Area Madaras
Your Child at Play (5 Volumes), by Marilyn Segal, Ph.D.

For more information, see our website www.newmarketpress.com

To my beautiful wife, Laura,
who coaxed, prodded, and supported me and stood by my side
at all times. I could not have written the book without her.

Acknowledgments

I wish to acknowledge my four sons who continue to teach me the meaning of having fun in all sports endeavors, as well as my parents and mother- and father-in-law for supporting me emotionally. I wish to acknowledge individual colleagues who have helped me with the preparation of the book and supported me: Donna Winters for her organizational skills; Tanya Termine for her computer proficiency; Ryan Lee for helping me with the strength and conditioning chapter; Noelle Sheehan for her input on sports nutrition; Mary Raine for her help on sports psychology; Dr. Jason Kronberg, my first fellow in sports medicine, for reviewing the illustrations and providing constructive ideas; my agent, Wendy Harrison Hashmall, who shared a common vision with me about the vital need for a book on kids and sports; the staff at Newmarket Press, including Keith Hollaman, Michelle Howry, and Shannon Berning, who did an excellent job in providing feedback and guidance throughout the whole process; and the medical staff of pediatrics, orthopedics, and rehab medicine at Mount Sinai and the medical staff at Blythedale Children's Hospital for encouraging me in my clinical and academic work. Finally, I would like to recognize the important role of my patients and their parents and the coaches, nurses, and physicians who I come in contact with on a daily basis who have asked the important questions.

Contents

PART III: COMMON QUESTIONS AND ANSWERS:
Preventive Medicine, Injury Rehabilitation, Nutrition, and Sports Psychology

Foreword

by Sheryl Swoopes

Professional Basketball Player on the WNBA Houston Comets
and Two-time Olympic Basketball Gold Medalist

I grew up in Brownfield, Texas, with my mother and three brothers—
James, Earl, and Brandon—and we have always been close. When I
was seven years old, my two older brothers James and Earl were playing basketball outside. I wanted to play with them, but I remember my
mother telling me to stay inside and play with my dolls. I really wanted
to play basketball, so I convinced my mother to let me play with them.
It was even harder to convince my brothers!

Of course, all kids should be going outside to play to stimulate their
interest in physical activity. Secondly, if a child is athletic he or she
should be encouraged to go for it. Coming from a close-knit family
taught me the importance of teamwork and the importance of everyone working together toward a common goal. I have used these lessons
that I learned as a young child—to rely on myself and my teammates—
through high school, college, and even in the WNBA.

In high school I participated in volleyball, track, and basketball. I
think playing all of these sports complemented each other. I never got

burnt out. I always looked forward to the next season because each sport was fun and I liked the competition.

I have worked very hard playing basketball in high school, college, the professional leagues in Italy, and currently with the Houston Comets. However, there have been many ups and downs, and when I was a child, there was no written athletic guide to help give me or my mother direction or advice. At the time, we didn't understand the importance of nutrition, hydration, injury prevention, and many other issues affecting young athletes. I have personally struggled with many of these same issues myself. There have been a couple of times since I've been in the WNBA when I didn't eat or drink properly, and I became dehydrated. This certainly affected my performance.

My time in college and with my coaches (Lyndon Hardin from South Plains Community College and Marsha Sharp from Texas Tech) definitely transformed me as a person and as a basketball player. However, it wasn't until training in the 1996 Olympics in Atlanta that I realized that I had to work extra hard on my fitness to be the best that I could be. Hopefully many young athletes can learn the importance of fitness and conditioning in junior high or high school.

This past year, I tore my knee up. It takes time to get one's mental confidence and physical strength back. When I suffered the knee injury, back in April of 2001, many thoughts went through my mind. I thought my career might be over. I believe if I had better knowledge in these areas, I might have had an easier time developing as an athlete and, subsequently, recovering from injuries. Having proper guidance as a child can set the proper tone for life.

Having a book like *Kids & Sports* would have been great when I was growing up, especially the chapters on nutrition and training. This book is perfect for parents, coaches, and players from all walks of life—whether they have all the money and resources in the world or don't have much money at all. *Kids & Sports* will be a great guide while I raise my five-year-old son, Jordan. One message from the book, which scores the winning basket, is to have fun and work hard whatever you do in life.

Introduction

My whole life in some way or another has been related to kids and sports. I can vividly remember when I was eleven years old and a star little league pitcher. After one particularly exciting game, I complained to my mom of severe pain at the inner side of my elbow. She brought me to the local bone specialist (there was no such thing as pediatric sports medicine back then). He told my mom and me that I should never pitch again. He offered no other specific advice or treatment. I was devastated by his statement, but as advised, I never pitched again. I continued to play baseball, and later took up tennis, but to this day, I wonder *What if* . . .

I know now that I suffered from Little League Elbow, a condition that is common in Little League pitchers and characterized by pain and inflammation of the growing bone, muscle, and tendons in the elbow. The treatment is no pitching for four to twelve weeks, as well as arm strengthening and flexibility exercises and then a gradual resumption of pitching. (The diagnosis of no more pitching forever is outrageous!) This personal experience has shaped my lifelong goal of helping children and families deal with sports injuries and medical conditions to allow them to fully participate in sports whenever appropriate.

I have played sports all of my life—I played high school baseball and tennis, and was a star varsity tennis player in college. I have coached young athletes since I was fifteen, and I continue to do so today. I am married and have four sons—ages eight, six, four, and eighteen months. I have taught and coached them in various sports. My professional specialty is pediatric/adolescent sports medicine, which means I take care of young athletes who have suffered from a sports injury, parents who want advice about appropriate sports for their child, or young athletes who want to get back into sports after an injury or with a medical condition.

Imagine a group of parents at a neighborhood barbeque who ask one another:

"Does your town have good youth soccer?

"Are you signing Jessica up for ballet lessons or karate?"

"Michael sprained his ankle last week; do you think he can play in tonight's game?"

In the last decade of the twentieth century, we witnessed a huge emphasis on youth sports and physical activities. Currently, there are 30 million children participating in individual and group sports—an increase of 10 million in the past six years. Not only are there more children involved with leagues, teams, and individual activities, but also, children are becoming more competitive at an earlier age. It is not uncommon for a child to begin ballet, swimming, tennis, gymnastics, or ice skating by age three or four.

Yet, we should ask: Are sports and physical activities being taught and performed with the well-being—present and future—of the children uppermost in our minds? Or, are we pushing them too far, too fast?

Children are not miniature adults; they are physiologically and psychologically different. These differences can impact their ability to perform specific athletic skills and have an influence on the frequency and severity of their injuries. Only recently have parents and coaches begun to recognize the myriad of medical issues surrounding children and sports.

Consider the difference one decade has made in child-oriented activities. One generation ago there were no "play dates," "Mommy and Me" classes, or "Gymboree" play areas. Nor were there rock-climbing birthday parties, soccer leagues for four-year-olds, or specialty sports camps for children under the age of ten. Gone are the days of simple pickup basketball or baseball games on sandlots or neighborhood parks.

As we enter the new millennium, we recognize that parents lack adequate information regarding appropriate athletic activities for their children. They simply do not know what sports are suitable for which age, what strategies offer protection against injury, or how to plan sports programs for children with chronic conditions (asthma, diabetes, neuromuscular disability, etc.). Current trends, family, friends, and even ego are unfortunately driving these decisions.

We all know that physical activity is vital for all children, yet there are few written sources for parents that offer objective, commonsense advice. My lifelong love of sports and working with children combined with my profession give me unique perspective on offering advice for children and their parents. I hope this book serves as a guide for enjoyable sports participation and allows young athletes to perform their best at their chosen sport.

PART I

YOUR YOUNG ATHLETE:

Skill Development and
Sports Selection

CHAPTER ONE

THE YOUNGEST ATHLETES:
Birth Through Age Five

Kathy had a son who, at fourteen months, was not yet walking. She voiced concerns about this to me on several occasions. Her other two children both walked at ten months and were very athletic. Was this a sign, she wondered, of her youngest son's future behavior? Would he be lazy and uninterested in sports?

Every parent wants his or her child to be healthy, and a big part of health is physical activity and motor development. I reassured Kathy that her son had not failed at motor development. Her baby was just growing at his own speed. The average child walks at around twelve months of age. The range, however, is nine to sixteen months, and the age at which a baby begins to walk has no influence on future athletic prowess.

INFANTS: BIRTH TO EIGHTEEN MONTHS

Babies start moving during the very first days of life. Movement is how they begin to explore and interact with their surroundings. It is also the time for your future athlete to begin building an important foundation—to learn that being physically active is essential for a healthy life.

There are two types of play and stimulation that all babies need: (1) interaction with a caregiver, and (2) exploration on their own. I believe an infant with these two different styles of play will develop her brain and intellect quicker, and will have an increased chance of growing into a more active child.

The first and best way for a baby to learn that exercise is a lifetime routine is by emulating her parents. You should be your child's role model, incorporating physical activity into your daily routine and involving your child in your workout routine whenever possible. It's great if you are already active, and you should continue to be—even though it is difficult with a newborn, and even tougher if you have additional kids. If you have not been exercising, this is a good time to start.

If weather permits, take your baby out for a walk everyday. It is good for everyone! Mom or Dad has a chance to exercise, and the baby will begin to associate these outdoor walks with physical activity. Later on, these walks will start to translate into an active outdoor playtime.

Indoor time is the place for your baby to work on her motor skills. A baby should not be placed in restrictive environments, such as car seats, cribs, or swings, for extended periods of time. Short periods of time are OK, but it is a good idea to move your baby to new play areas every so often. Restrictive environments for long stays might delay your child's gross motor skills—those integrated muscle actions that produce running, walking, throwing, and kicking. Instead, place your baby on the floor and play. You may gently move and massage your baby, and of course, always have fun!

Older siblings or other relatives closer to your baby's own age are important role models, too. It is important for your baby to see them run, throw, catch, and play tag. Infants are very imitative. They often roll their arms and kick legs as if running in place, and they frequently thrust their hands above their heads as if to throw.

Infant toys are critical to the development of motor skills. To further their development, babies should have toys that they can reach out and grasp. The list below gives some games, toys, and activities that are enjoyable for your infant.

Activities for Your Infant

- Babies really enjoy holding a ball in their hands, especially when they see their older siblings play with it. Take a tennis ball, whiffle ball, football, basketball—basically any ball that a baby sees his parents or older siblings playing with—and roll it back and forth. Babies think this is lots of fun, and it will guarantee baby belly laughs.
- Small sports toys, such as a minibasketball, a minibaseball, a baby-size bat, a small soccer ball, or a rubber infant-sized tennis racket can set the tone for an active childhood. Large beach balls can be a lot of fun for your baby, too.
- After your infant can stand, hold her hands up and walk with her. This helps develop her strength. Also, babies love to copy what their parents are doing, and they feel proud of themselves.
- When your child is walking, offer her push-and-pull toys. This will stimulate her to explore her environment and further develop her motor skills.

TODDLERS: AGES EIGHTEEN MONTHS TO THREE YEARS

Toddlers are beginning to really establish their fundamental gross motor skills: walking, running, jumping, hopping, and skipping. As with an infant, toddlers still require adult interaction to help with their physical activity, but they also need time to explore on their own. Toddlers should be exposed to at least thirty minutes a day of physical activity. Children this age still have short attention spans, so placing your child in an organized sport (such as soccer) with complicated rules to follow would probably not be effective.

A mix of both structured and unstructured physical activities should be planned for your child. There's a distinction between organized sports and structured activities. The mixture of activities will produce a child who is more interested in his environment and will efficiently acquire motor skills and master them. *Structured activities* include classes for which you register your child—gymnastics, swim team, or dance lessons, for example—compared to just kicking or throwing a ball around with your child. *Unstructured activities* are what this age group loves the most—just plain having fun and running around. Playgrounds are great for developing motor skills. "Mommy and Me" classes that have indoor play equipment are also good.

As your child plays, remember to establish a safe play area—one that is level, free of small objects a toddler can swallow, and free of sharp edges. This way your youngster will gain confidence as she develops her new skills. Also, join your child in her games and activities. This will offer her encouragement as well as stimulating her abilities.

Activities for Your Toddler

- Children love to move, sway, and dance to music. Dance movements teach kids how to move, while simultaneously encouraging creativity and imagination, all of which are important in sports.
- If you use exercise tapes at home, have your toddler watch you. Let him jump around while you are getting your exercise. And, since toddlers learn best with repetitive activity, the tapes can be used over and over again without your toddler getting bored.
- Get outside! Play catch with your toddler, and let him throw, kick, and play run-and-chase games like tag and hide-and-seek.
- Large inflatable balls to toss around are still loads of fun for toddlers.
- Playground sets are great, because they allow kids to push, pull, crawl, climb, and safely jump. Just be sure to monitor your children closely while they're playing.
- In the summertime, splashing around in a wading pool is

wonderful for kids. I generally do not recommend swim safety classes—these often give children and their parents a false sense of security around water. An adult should always have the child in full view until the child can fully swim; never leave your child alone near the water. A child can drown in even six inches of water.

PRESCHOOLERS: AGES THREE TO FIVE

Children of preschool age are beginning to refine their movements, and they are using more complex motor skills for longer periods of time. Preschoolers move with great energy as they explore their surroundings. They alternate between bursts of energy and short periods of rest.

These kids are beginning to throw and kick, and they are putting together more sophisticated movement skills. They can now run, jump, and change direction quickly. These patterns set the stage for movement in sports, such as basketball, soccer, tennis, and hockey. In addition, preschool-age kids are beginning to judge distances, although not to the point of perfection. It is a delight to watch these kids revel in their new accomplishments.

Preschoolers can now take direction and instruction for short periods of time, and could begin organized sports like soccer or gymnastics. These classes typically teach skill development rather than emphasizing rules. It is a good idea to start exposing your child to a variety of sports to see what type of sport your child will like.

Children at this age are most often attending nursery school or preschool. Look for preschool programs that enrich the curriculum with physical activities. Having appropriate indoor and outdoor play spaces are critical to your child's development. Physical activity and vigorous playtime should be scheduled each day in the preschool program.

Preschoolers are also beginning to use athletic equipment. Large soccer balls (size 3 or 4), whiffle balls, soft baseballs, or junior-sized basketballs are appropriate. Hard baseballs, regulation basketballs, and adult-sized tennis rackets are *not* appropriate for preschoolers. It is important that this equipment is the right size. With properly sized equipment, children become better balanced and more nimble on their feet. If your child uses gear that is too big, she might become frustrated.

It is important to know your child's development. You need to challenge your child—make her successful but at the same time not make tasks and activities too difficult. If your child needs help in the park, offer your support and take her hand. Your child will develop at her own rate; do not compare her to any other child. Some kids take longer to develop and some kids are quicker. You have to know what is developmentally appropriate and what would be the most fun for your child.

Activities for Your Preschooler

- Simple ball games, such as kickball, teach children a variety of skills involving rolling, kicking, throwing, and catching.
- Group games, such as hide-and-seek, musical chairs, duck-duck-goose, and freeze tag, are good for stimulating an interest in running.
- Riding on scooters and on tricycles are developmentally appropriate activities that use complex motor patterns. Properly sized bicycle helmets should always be worn for scooter and tricycle riding. For scooters, wrist, elbow, and knee guards are recommended.
- Throwing balls into hoops or buckets develops throwing skills and upper body coordination.
- Jumping, hopping, and running encourage balance and coordination. Games like tag, Simon Says, and hide-and-seek may incorporate these movements. Games like Simon Says and limbo help children link directions to actual movement.

Q&A WITH DR. SMALL

Q*My three-year-old is great at soccer. He runs and kicks the ball like a much older child. Do you think I should start developing his skills, and do you think he could become an elite athlete?*

A Your child might indeed become an elite athlete, but at this age it is far too early to tell. I am an advocate of athletic activity at an early age, but competitive sports require more physical and emotional development than a three-year-old can handle. It is usually not before the age of eight that children can fully understand the concept of teamwork and sharing strategies. I generally do not recommend specializing in one sport year-round before the age of twelve.

I suggest that you expose your son to other sports so he has choices. You might be raising the next Michael Jordan or Tiger Woods, but with few exceptions, most great athletes have overall developmental growth before they devote themselves to one sport. John McEnroe played soccer and basketball in high school, in addition to his tennis games. Tim Duncan of the San Antonio Spurs was a national-level swimmer and did not play basketball until late high school.

Q*Do children naturally learn fundamental motor skills, or must these skills be taught?*

A Many people believe that fundamental motor skills evolve naturally, but I don't believe this is true. I believe children may perform these skills at the appropriate age, but they don't necessarily advance to a more mature level without instruction and practice. Physical activity with solid support promotes emotional, social, physical, and intellectual development, which becomes the foundation for what will follow in each child's life.

Q My three-year-old shows promise in sports. But he has flat feet and is significantly intoeing when he is walking. Is there anything I can do for his feet?

A Anatomic abnormalities tend to be family traits. *Intoeing* is a condition in which the toes on each foot turn inward and the heels are turned outward. Either Mom or Dad probably intoes and has flat feet. Intoeing might slightly correct itself later on, but the tendency to intoe will never go away. For these cases, stretching and strengthening exercises can be helpful. The good news is that flat feet or intoeing will have no effect on strength or running speed, and will not predispose your child to injury.

Q I want to start my three-year-old in gymnastics. There are so many programs to choose from. How do I make a good choice?

A You must look for a program that has a small student-to-teacher ratio, with child-friendly instructors. Of course, these instructors need to be qualified. You can call the different programs in your area and speak with the director regarding the philosophy of the program (playful vs. regimented), the experience of the instructors, and the variety of activities.

My own children started gymnastics at a highly rated academy, but I was not satisfied with the program. This particular program did not give the children enough individual attention—only the one or two outstanding young gymnasts received adequate attention. After speaking with some parents, I discovered another academy that was better suited for my children. Don't be afraid to move your child if you are not satisfied with the program.

Q I have two-year-old twins. At what age do you recommend they begin swim lessons?

A Between the ages of two and three is an excellent time to begin swim lessons, especially if they have expressed an interest.

Swimming helps kids to establish control over their body movements. If you find that your children are reluctant to swim, however, then I would wait until they seem more comfortable with the idea. Learning how to swim is indeed important, but it's also important for your children to begin swimming when they are mature enough to learn the necessary skills.

Q We live in a large city, and I am looking at preschools for my three-year-old. Many schools in my area do not have outdoor playgrounds. Should this be a consideration as I make my final decision?

A I would urge you to choose a program that makes physical activity an important part of its program. This is an important time for preschool-age children as they develop their gross motor skills, and preschoolers need to run around. If the school does not have an outdoor playground, an indoor playground or a rooftop playground could be a possible substitute. But more important than the size of the school's playground is that the teacher express an interest in physical activity, and that this be imparted onto the children.

Q How do you balance television habits with physical activity?

A The American Academy of Pediatrics has taken a strong position on this matter. They recommend that children under two years of age do not watch television. The first two years of life are crucial in developing your child's concentration, creativity, and independence. These qualities are necessary for sports and everyday life. When children begin to watch television, it is important to limit how much they watch everyday. In my house, I limit the TV time to one hour a day, and my children can watch only after they have finished all their physical activities, homework, and other household jobs. If my kids do not have a scheduled sport planned, then they must go outside to play. The motto in our household is, "If it's light outside, we're outside"—weather permitting, of course.

Q We live in a large city and there are no playgrounds nearby. How else can I engage my children in physical activity?

A We'd all like a stretch of green lawn in our backyard for our children to play in, but sometimes that is just not the reality. With a little creativity, though, even urban kids can get the physical activity they need to stay healthy. You and your child can engage in activities in your apartment, such as putting music on and dancing around. And just because you're inside doesn't mean you can't play with Nerf balls or balloons—particularly with younger children. Walking is also good physical activity that you can all do together while you run errands. Finally, look into your neighborhood community center and see if it offers indoor activities.

CHAPTER TWO

THE SCHOOL-AGE ATHLETE:
Six to Eleven Years

One day, Sharon spoke to me with great concern. Her son was seven, and Sharon was trying very hard to interest him in a variety of sport activities. Her son had tried soccer, tennis, swimming, floor hockey, and was now getting ready to try gymnastics. She wanted him to be exposed to as many sports as possible, so he could then choose the one or two that he liked best. But Sharon was weary. "There are too many choices," she told me.

Sharon's story typifies the increasing sport choices that are offered to youngsters in the school-age group (ages six to eleven.) In this family's case, I suggested to Sharon that her son had tried enough—perhaps it was time to concentrate on the one or two sports that he already had expressed interest in.

The benefits of sports activities for kids are undeniable. In addition to the health benefits, youngsters involved in sports typically will have higher academic scores. In addition, these children will typically have improved "social intelligence," which will lead to longer ongoing friendships. For girls in particular, the confidence gained is especially important once they hit middle school and high school. Girls, most often, drop out of sports at this age if they are not encouraged.

School-age children now have the basic skills necessary to begin playing any sport of their choosing. The choices for these kids are endless, including organized sports (soccer, baseball, tennis, swimming) or other athletic pursuits (skiing, bicycling, bowling, fencing). These school-age athletes fit in two age groups: (1) children ages six to eight and (2) children ages eight to eleven.

EARLY ELEMENTARY SCHOOL: AGES SIX TO EIGHT

Children ages six to eight are beginning to master more complex sports skills. These kids have now mastered most elements of adult throwing and kicking skills, although most still cannot put together two skills, such as throwing and running at the same time. By age six, learning how to swim or mastering a two-wheel bike become important milestones.

It is crucial for youngsters to practice their newfound skills in order to gain proficiency in sports. Their cognitive thinking has now developed to the point that they can actively learn how to improve their movements. For example, a child learning how to kick a soccer ball can cognitively learn the moves needed to improve her kick. With diligent practice, children can keep improving until they have a terrific game by the age of nine or ten.

At the same time, their improved motor skills should lead children to experiment with many different kinds of sports. Your child may be practicing dribbling a basketball one day and playing catch the next. At this age, it is best to avoid organized programs that emphasize winning over enjoyment and skill acquisition. By involving your kid in activities that are fun, you'll be promoting a lifetime of physical activity.

Sport Selection

You should assist your child in selecting sports activities based on his physical and emotional strengths. Some of this is common sense: If your child is short in stature and low in weight, it's wise to steer him to sports or other physical activities that do not rely on height and body weight. Such sports include racquet sports, martial arts, baseball, and soccer. This child should be shifted away from contact sports (hockey, football) where weight definitely confers an advantage.

For the larger-framed child, contact sports such as basketball, hockey, football, or lacrosse would be fine. This is not to say that a slight-framed child cannot succeed in hockey or that a larger-framed child cannot succeed in karate. However, a child's body type definitely presents inherent advantages for some sports and disadvantages for others. Children and their parents should pay attention to their natural strengths and weaknesses.

Parents must also take into account their child's personality when selecting a sport. Again, recognizing your child's natural strengths and preferences can help you to choose a sport that she'll really "click" with. Some children, like some adults, prefer working alone rather than working with others. These kids will probably enjoy sports such as tennis, golf, or running rather than team sports such as basketball, soccer, or football. Some sports, such as baseball, fall into both camps—though a child is part of a team, she is basically flying solo when she's up to bat.

Sport Specialization

For the majority of cases in this age group, it is too young to specialize in one sport. The disadvantages of specialization can be burnout, frustration, and injury. The only advantage to concentrating on just one sport at this age would be in highly technical sports such as gymnastics or figure skating, where endless repetition is the key to success. Even with gymnastics or figure skating, it is a good idea for kids to try other sports, as exposure to a wider variety of sports would most likely complement a child's success. For example, soccer or basketball, which both involve a great deal of running and or jumping, may translate into more explosive actions in gymnastics and figure skating.

Games to Play With Your Child

- Practice throwing balls through hoops, baskets, or at targets. This is good for eye-hand coordination and will be needed for specific sports such as tennis, racquet ball, field hockey, lacrosse, and volleyball.
- Kicking soccer balls or beach balls helps with movement and gross motor development, and it is useful for soccer skill development.
- Playing tag games are still fun for kids of this age, and this helps to improve agility.
- Practice batting or striking objects with bats, racquets, or paddles. Take a soft tennis ball and have your child bat it or strike it with a racquet.

LATE ELEMENTARY SCHOOL: AGES EIGHT TO ELEVEN

Children ages eight to eleven have nearly mastered more complex sport skills and can now use them to play organized sports. They can put a set of complex motor skills together, like running, jumping, cutting (quickly changing direction and weaving side to side), throwing, and kicking, and can make use of these skills in the context of a sports game or practice. Such skills should be practiced in a variety of settings: at home, with friends, in an official practice, and during sports games. In addition, these skills need to be demonstrated by teammates, adults, and coaches.

At the same time, the intellect of kids of this age is more fully developed—they can now begin to understand the concepts of sharing, passing, and strategizing. As opposed to ages five to seven, where children all swarm toward the ball, these children now understand teamwork and can anticipate their teammates' or opponents' moves.

Children ages eight to eleven love games, and they enjoy improving their skills. It is important that you practice skill improvement with them—activities like shooting hoops, playing catch, hitting a baseball, or kicking a soccer ball are all good. Your child will benefit, and you both will have fun. I still remember my father pitching to me (at first a whiffle ball, then a tennis ball, and finally a baseball) while I practiced my batting skills. Those were bonding moments for us, and I encourage you to do the same. The free time spent with your child will pay huge dividends in terms of forming a parent/child bond, but also by demonstrating that you, the adult, value sports and physical activity.

Do not forget that children still want to play for fun. It is critical for children in this age group to have positive experiences with sports and sports programs. By age eleven, more than half of children have quit organized sports. Kids cite several common reasons for quitting:

- Sports cease to be fun.
- Sports become too competitive.
- She does not receive enough playing time.

When children in this age group have positive experiences in sports, the rewards can have far-reaching consequences. Kids who play sports experience camaraderie with others, learn leadership skills, and tend to develop enhanced self-esteem. A nine-, ten-, or eleven-year-old who has mastered basketball, soccer, baseball, or tennis skills may help out a team of six- or seven-year-olds in a chosen sport. He may even teach his younger siblings, neighbors, or cousins; in so doing, he takes on the role as teacher/mentor and reaffirms his interest in sports.

Sports Selection

As with the six- to eight-year-old group, sports selection for eight- to eleven-year-olds often depends upon physical attributes such as size and weight. However, the physical maturity of the child comes into play here as well. Some ten- or eleven-year-old boys or nine- or ten-year-old girls are early maturers who are almost fully grown. These children are more likely to succeed in strength or contact sports. The late-maturing children are more likely to succeed in activities where height and weight don't matter or may even pose a disadvantage (gymnastics or figure skating, for example). But that's not to say that there's no mobility for your child once she selects a sport—in my practice, I have a number of excellent figure skaters who started as gymnasts but switched to skating after they "outgrew" gymnastics. In other sports (racquet sports, running), height and weight pose neither an advantage nor a disadvantage.

In addition, the personality traits of a child should be taken into account. A large-framed boy could actually dislike more aggressive contact sports like football or rugby, even though he is physically suited for them. In this case, it would be wise to gear him toward a noncontact activity. One family in my practice has two sons—the oldest likes contact sports even though he is not large bodied, and the younger boy, while large for his age, prefers to avoid contact and aggression. Make sure the activities you select are a good physical and psychological fit for your child. It's only logical: If a child enjoys a sport and feels comfortable while playing, he is more likely to stick with it.

Sport Specialization

You definitely know your child's strengths and interests. If your child shows particular promise or expertise in one sport, it's definitely a good idea to encourage that interest. But at the same time, keep her involved in other activities. I don't think that the majority of children are physically or emotionally mature enough to specialize in one sport year round until they are eleven or twelve. Before this age, children often lack the attention span and dedication to concentrate on one activity (of course, there are exceptions).

Games to Play With Your Child

- Shooting baskets
- Playing pitch and catch
- Kicking the soccer ball

- Playing two against one in basketball, soccer, hockey can be entertaining for all family members involved.

Children who do not enjoy organized sports can try the following activities:

- Hiking
- Biking
- Inline skating
- Walking
- Ice Skating
- Skateboarding

Many children in this age group start dropping out of organized sports and do not continue with physical activity of any kind. Team sports have become too competitive for them, and when they stop having fun they quit altogether. Part of the problem is the structure of today's society, which does not allow youngsters the opportunity for much free playtime. Children often find themselves in games or practices that are organized and supervised by adults who place too much pressure on their children. Don't schedule every minute of your child's day—give him free time to play. And remember to make "family time" for more unstructured physical activities like walking, bike riding, or hiking with your kids on a regular basis. This helps you, and them, to reestablish a commitment to an active lifestyle.

Below is a table that may be helpful in choosing sports activities for your child. A few things to remember:

- When deciding at what age your child should begin a sport, always take into account your child's particular physical and mental abilities. These are only recommended ages to start the sport through classes, instruction, or clinics. Some children may be able to start earlier or later depending on their physical and mental maturity. The most important goals at these young ages are having fun and learning motor skills.

- "Concentrating" means specializing in one sport. While the chart below gives the recommended ages for concentrating on different sports, I am a firm believer of exposing a child to as many sports and physical activities as possible. Even in the teenage years playing more than one sport is recommended.

SPORTS SELECTION—WHICH SPORT IS RIGHT FOR MY CHILD?				
Sport	Physical Abilities	Mental Abilities	Age to Start	Age to Concentrate
Baseball	Good eye-hand coordination	Concentration	Age 6 for some fundamental skills, such as throwing, fielding, and catching	14
Basketball	Quickness, height, jumping ability	Ability to make quick decisions, ability to share (teamwork)	6–8	14
Football	Strength	Ability to deal with pain, aggressiveness	7–8	18 or upon entering college
Golf	Body control, balance	Focus, dedication, concentration	6–8	10–12
Figure skating	Muscular flexibility, technical proficiency	Dedication, hard work	3–5	8–10
Gymnastics	Muscular flexibility, technical proficiency	Dedication, hard work	3–5	8–10
Fencing	Body control, quickness	Concentration, intelligence	10–12	14–16

Sport	Physical Abilities	Mental Abilities	Age to Start	Age to Concentrate
Tennis	Good hand-eye coordination, quickness, agility	Focus, concentration	7–8	12–14
Hockey	Muscle strength	Aggressiveness	6–8	12–15
Swimming	Muscle strength, endurance	Hard work	4–6	12–14
Running	Muscle explosiveness for sprinting, endurance for distance	Hard work, dedication	12–13	14–16
Lacrosse	Muscle strength, running ability	Aggressiveness, ability to tolerate and withstand physical contact	8	14
Soccer	Running ability, quickness	Ability to make quick decisions, teamwork, decisiveness	5–6	12–14
Skiing	Muscle balance, strength, balance	Concentration, decisiveness	4–6	12–14

Q&A WITH DR. SMALL

Q My seven-year-old son has dropped out of soccer, but all his friends are still playing. Does this mean that my son will not be good in any type of organized sport? Should I try more individual activities, or should I try baseball?

A Just because your son does not like soccer does not mean he's a failure at organized sports. His soccer team may have been too competitive, or perhaps he simply didn't like running after the ball. Try another sport with him, such as baseball, which is very different from soccer. You should certainly encourage him to try other team sports, especially if he expresses an interest. Of course, there are also individual sports he can try, such as martial arts or skateboarding. Speak to your son and see what he wants to do. Listening to what he wants is the most important factor in helping him find the right sport.

Q *My eleven-year-old son wants to go on a twenty-mile bike trip with his father. He's never gone on such a long trip before, although he rides his bike around the neighborhood. Is this long trip OK for him, or should he be building up for this day?*

A The answer depends on how far he's traveled on the bike before. If he's only been riding in the neighborhood, which might be about a mile or so, then perhaps the outing should be postponed until your son has done lengthier bike trips. Your son should build up to a long ride like this—traveling one mile a few times, then riding for five miles, then ten, and then fifteen until he is comfortable riding the twenty miles with your husband. It might take some time for your son to be prepared to ride this distance. If he has completed five- to ten-mile bike outings in the past, he could very well be ready to go the distance a lot sooner. You will want your husband to arrange for a water break or snack every fifteen minutes to prevent dehydration or potential injury.

Q *My eight-year-old daughter has never played competitive sports before. This year, she wants to play for the town soccer team. Are there any special precautions she should take or things I should be aware of before enrolling her?*

A It's great thing that your daughter wants to try a new sport. If this team holds practices and plays only one time a week, then she probably doesn't need any special preparation. If the team is more serious and plays more often, then some practice with friends or a coach may be needed to build her endurance and stamina.

I would be cautious about how competitive this team is. Remember, many of these kids probably have been playing soccer for some time. The ideal situation would be a league in which the children play in friendly competition, with teams that have children with a variety of skill levels. But if the competition is fierce or the children are all advanced, then this activity might to be too forceful for an eight-year-old with little experience.

Q My nine-year-old daughter is very intelligent, yet she is not interested in sports. How can I raise her interest?

A Your goal should not necessarily be to have your daughter on a competitive team, but to find one or more recreational activities that she can do for a lifetime. These activities may include hiking, biking, walking, inline skating, or swimming. The best way to encourage your daughter is for the two of you to pick an activity to do together and to do it on a regular basis. Set aside part of one day on the weekend and let that become your sport time. As your daughter gains interest, the two of you might gradually add another day to your sporting routine, and perhaps you both might vary the activity.

Q My nine-year-old daughter was recently moved up in gymnastics from level six to seven. She told me that her coach wants her to increase her practice time from four hours a week to twelve hours a week. I think this is too much. What do you think?

A If your daughter enjoys gymnastics, then increasing her weekly training is fine. Children who try to achieve national recognition in this sport must put in long hours.

However, I do think that training for four hours per week and jumping up to twelve hours per week is too big of a leap at one time. This is an increase of 300 percent! Your daughter should slowly increase her training schedule at intervals of 10 to 20 percent, until she reaches the desired goal of twelve hours per week. In addition to increasing the risk of burnout, training too hard and too fast often leads to an increased risk of overuse or acute injury. See Chapter Eleven: Common Sports Injuries for additional information.

Q *What is the best age for a child to begin competitive sports?*

A The best age to start your child in competitive sports is between the ages of seven and eight. Before this age, children have not yet developed the skills or concentration needed in organized sports. These kids usually do not have a lengthy attention span and do not fully understand the concepts of passing and teamwork.

Q *My eight-year-old son is scheduled for soccer twice a week, for karate one day a week, and for swim lessons one day a week. Do you think he is overinvolved?*

A The answer to this question depends upon your child. If he is happy and if his skills are improving, then your son is not doing too many activities. If, however, your son complains that he is fatigued, tired, or bored, or if your son begins to complain of unexplained joint pain, then your son might very well be overextended. If this is the situation, then your son's schedule should be scaled back.

Q *My daughter, age ten, is very athletic and wants to do gymnastics competitively. But surprisingly, she's never even tried it before. How should we approach this?*

A I would never discourage a child to start a new activity, but I don't think your daughter can be competitive right away. First, she would need to learn the basics of gymnastics. Enroll your daughter in a gymnastics academy, see how she likes the program, and then see what her coaches say.

Q My eight-year-old son wants to play tackle football for the first time. My wife thinks it is much too dangerous at this age and wants him to wait until high school to play such a tough sport. What do you think?

A All research studies show that football has the highest injury rate among all sports. If your son plans to play football, the safest time to begin is at age eight, nine, or ten. This is because most boys of this age are relatively the same size and the same weight. They cannot run that fast, and they cannot generate much power in a tackling maneuver.

However, as children grow older (fourteen or fifteen), their size, speed, and strength vary greatly. Those who are slight in size are at a distinct disadvantage for contact sports like football. If you son wants to try football, it's significantly safer at age eight than at age fourteen.

CHAPTER THREE

THE TEENAGE ATHLETE:
Twelve to Eighteen Years

Joshua, a lanky sixteen-year-old athlete, plays basketball year-round. He is six foot one inch and weighs just 140 pounds. Last year, as a junior, he played on the junior varsity team. His coach tells him that although he shows great promise, he needs to bulk up and get stronger to make the varsity next season. Although his parents considered him to be in excellent shape, they agreed to consult with a sports medicine specialist for specific guidance, nutritional advice, and a targeted weight-training program.

Last June, Mary, age seventeen, had her sports physical with me in preparation for her senior year in high school. During her visit, she mentioned an interest in running with the fall cross-country team. Although Mary is fit and agile and has played on several competitive teams, she and her mom wanted to know if there would be any special preparation Mary should do over the summer prior to tryouts.

Brendan, a fourteen-year-old straight-A student and a self-proclaimed "couch potato," has never participated in any

exercise or organized sports before. He will be entering his fresh-man year in high school. His parents have been watching Bren-dan's growing frame turn to soft tissue and told him that he should join a sport or pick up some exercise for conditioning his body during his continued growth. One Thursday, they came to me as a family to help Brendan tone his body to the same level as his mind.

All of the above scenarios represent the many issues confronting teens in sports. Likewise, in my practice, I've noticed three different kinds of high school kids:

- The star athlete, who specializes in one sport
- The avid recreational athlete
- The non-athlete

The issues discussed in this chapter target each type of teenager, and how to improve sports performance, how to prepare for a new sport, and how to help beginners begin a new sport and/or exercise program.

As a parent you know what type of child you have.

THE STAR ATHLETE

Today, many teen athletes want to reach the varsity level in high school and may even be contemplating playing their preferred sport in college. (Parents might be thinking the same thing, hoping for a college scholarship.) What these kids have in common is their desire to reach their greatest potential.

Improving Sports Performance

A good way to begin to improve sports performance is to complete the following exercise with your child. It's a good idea to ask the coach for help and guidance because the coach can often be objective.

- *Make a list of physical strengths and weaknesses.* For example, how fast does your child run, how agile is she, how much muscle strength does she exhibit?
- *List yearly goals.* For example, does your child want to run the mile in under six minutes? Does he want to hit six home runs? Does she want to score twenty points in one basketball game?
- *List any cross training, weight training, and agility training that your child is currently doing.* For example, is your teenager swimming and biking in preparation for the upcoming cross-country running season? Is your teen doing free weights and resistance bands, or just push-ups and sit-ups? Is he doing footwork drills, like shuffling from side to side or running backwards?
- *List general nutritional habits, before, during, and after competition.* Is a healthy pregame meal eaten two to three hours prior to competition? Are healthy snacks packed and eaten during competition? Is the postgame meal adequate in total calories, especially carbohydrates and protein?
- *List fluid intake before, during, and after competition.* Is your teen drinking eight ounces of fluids (sport drinks, water, or diluted fruit drinks) beyond thirst level prior to competition?
- *List mental strengths and weaknesses.* Is your teenager confident or insecure? Does she have the killer instinct, or does she choke under pressure?

Once your teen completes this questionnaire, evaluates his strengths and weaknesses, and then begins to follow the ideas mentioned above, you should see results within six months or so, after which your child will be on the way towards achieving his personal best sports performance!

THE RECREATIONAL ATHLETE

Many teenagers are avid recreational athletes who enjoy the camaraderie and the competition that various sports offer. Once these active children reach the seventh, eighth, or ninth grade they often become interested in trying a new sport. If a friend says, "Hey, let's try tennis or volleyball; it looks like fun," your teen may very well take up the challenge. These kids have now become more secure and confident, and look forward to these new challenges. At this point in time they might also become more serious in one sport or multiple sports.

Unlike figure skating or gymnastics, which take years to develop, the majority of the sports that I recommend below have skills that can be quickly acquired. I have not included baseball or soccer because most children begin these sports at a young age (most towns offer T-ball and soccer in kindergarten) and have been playing for many years. In some of these sports, such as crew or field events, all of the kids are at the same beginner level, which offers them an opportunity to advance their skills as a group, making the activity more fun and social.

Running	Badminton
Tennis	Lacrosse
Football	Volleyball
Wrestling	Crew
Fencing	Archery
Pole vaulting	Shot Put
Javelin	Discus

In order to prevent injury and to optimize sports performance, certain planning and precautions should be taken. It's a good idea to review with your teen the following tips:

- Don't train or practice too many hours right away.
- Learn proper technique through coaching and clinics if possible.
- Use proper equipment.
- Recognize the difference between muscle soreness and pain.
- Use common sense and know when to stop.
- Pick a practice partner.
- Speak with the coach to find out what skills to practice.

As an example, let's take the case of Mary, our seventeen-year-old girl who wants to begin fall cross-country running for the first time. Mary has a friend on the team, and she thought it would be fun to join her. Since she has never run long distances before, I recommended she start running six to eight weeks before the first official practice starts. Mary should start out at a slow running pace and at a distance she's comfortable with, perhaps one mile. She should run every other day for several weeks, and should start on a soft surface such as paved track or grass, never on concrete or on the road. She can increase her mileage by 10 percent to 20 percent per week. It is common to have soreness and minor aches and pains in knees, shins, and ankles the first several days. If pain persists for more than a week, her running should be decreased by 50 percent until the pain subsides.

While keeping the list mentioned above in mind, the recommendations for Mary are as follows: (1) Be sure to buy appropriate running shoes (don't run in your basketball or tennis shoes). Her footwear should have a well-cushioned heel and supportive arch. (2) Drink eight ounces of fluid beyond her thirst level, fifteen to thirty minutes prior to the run. (3) Speak with the coach regarding any other training recommendations or expectations (i.e., push-ups or sit-ups). (4) Keep a training log of daily, weekly, and monthly times and distances.

THE NON-ATHLETE

I see two kinds of non-athletes in my practice. There is the teenager who is reluctant to participate in all sports, despite encouragement from his parents. And there is the teen who might participate in sports but only under the right circumstances. Yet, despite these situations, it is important to get these kids motivated and moving so they can enjoy a lifelong habit, promoting good health. Girls' physical activity and fitness often starts to decrease at age twelve, so it's important get them interested as early as possible.

Some teens have never had a positive sport experience. Since both types of non-athletes do not generally yearn to be on any sports team, it is more appropriate for them to try something noncompetitive. There are many sports and activities to try, such as jogging, hiking, tennis, biking, walking, golf, swimming, inline skating, or martial arts. However, the right situation could change your teenager's attitude. I encourage you to keep trying different ideas until some sport clicks with your child.

These non-athletes must be taught that exercise has great physical and mental benefits. You must explain to your child that regular exercise is good for him and it will improve his muscle strength, heart and lung fitness, bone density, and overall emotional well-being. Hopefully, by stressing these positive attributes, your teenager will begin a sport or exercise program. Remember, it's OK for your teen to start small. A small step will hopefully lead to a bigger one. For example, your teen can go out for a daily walk or bike ride. This might lead to tennis lessons, golf, or something else.

Local recreational leagues such as the YMCA, the local Boys and Girls Club, or the JCC community center offer many different kinds of activities for a teenager to make a new start.

Someone told me a story about coaching a girl's seventh and eighth grade soccer team. The coach said while some girls have been playing soccer for many years, there were an equal number of girls who have never tried soccer before. I think that's terrific! The atmosphere was noncompetitive, and the coach just wanted the girls to have fun.

INFORMATION FOR ALL TEENAGERS

Whether your child is a star athlete, a recreational athlete, or a non-athlete, it is important for your family to be active together. Skiing may be done in winter. Hiking and biking may be done in fall, spring, and summer. Involve your teenager in the decision-making process about what she wants to do and where she wants to go. Other activities such as miniature golf and bowling can be done on a more sporadic basis. These activities are fun for all ages and do not require much athletic prowess.

Q&A WITH DR. SMALL

How much physical activity should a teenager get?

Every teenager should participate in daily physical activity. The minimum for good health is exercising for twenty to thirty minutes with moderate intensity aerobic activity (biking, walking, jogging, swimming, or playing various ball games) at least three times per week. These activities should be continuous, although ten minutes two to three times per day would be adequate.

All of my son's fifteen-year-old friends are going to one- and two-week sports camps. I think that is too much—what do you think? Should I send him to a sports camp or a general camp?

You have several options here. First, you must find out what he wants to do. If he wants to do a one-week sports camp, then I would strongly consider his request. On the other hand, if he would prefer to attend a general camp, I would consider that as well. The best option may be to send him to a general camp as well as the sports camp, so he could have both experiences.

Q My fourteen-year-old son used to be very active in sports. Now he's in the ninth grade, and he's not good enough to make any of the high school sports teams. He would very much like to play, but there doesn't seem to be the opportunity. Do you have any suggestions?

A This does seem to be a dilemma, but I have several suggestions. Many towns (it could be your town or a neighboring town) have recreational leagues, which are not as competitive. In addition there are the local YMCA and community centers.

PART II

SPORTS FOR EVERY KID:

The Specific Needs of
Special Populations

CHAPTER FOUR

THE ELITE ATHLETE

Jen, a sixteen-year-old nationally ranked tennis player, has been a patient of mine for several years. Two years ago she came in for lower back pain. Within this same two-year period, I also treated Jen for shoulder pain, elbow pain, an ankle sprain, and an ankle stress fracture. There were concerns about her agility and about nutrition, which I evaluated as well. Jen's injuries were caused, we finally determined, because she played too many tennis tournaments. This summer, I recommended that Jen scale back to four tournaments. She was very successful and had a great injury-free summer.

WHAT IS AN ELITE ATHLETE?

When a youngster reaches a regional, national, or international level of competition in a sport, then he is considered an elite athlete. These youngsters train year-round, and because of this extensive training, the elite athlete needs a sports physician, a coach, and a team of health professionals: a nutritionist, a sports psychologist, a personal trainer, and a physical therapist. The elite athlete has special issues to consider, such as injury prevention and recovery, rest, nutrition, stress management, and training. Just as a baby often goes to the doctor, so

must the elite athlete maintain an ongoing relationship with his doctor, coach, and other health professionals.

TRAINING FOR THE ELITE ATHLETE

Of course, it is necessary for elite athletes to put in a great deal of
training—many more hours per week than the typical young athlete.
(Elite young athletes often train ten or more hours per week, whereas
recreational athletes usually train only two to eight hours per week.)
It is important to train hard, but the intensity of training should taper
off one to two weeks prior to competition. This is called periodization.
Without periodization, your child's muscles would be too sore and
tired to be effective. Muscles need to be revitalized for peak
performance.

While your child is in training, you should consider the following:

- *How much time should your child devote to practice sessions?*
  Practice sessions should constitute one half to one and a
  half times the competition hours. For example, if a young
  athlete has six hours of competition each week, then her
  practice should range from three to nine hours per week.
  The athlete should set daily, weekly, and yearly goals with
  a coach.
- *How can you keep your child's practice sessions interesting?* Practice sessions should vary in intensity, and playful challenges
  should be incorporated (e.g., How many baskets can you
  make in a row?).
- *How can you reinforce your child's strengths while practicing and
  improving her weak areas?* For example, a figure skater is good
  at jumping but needs help with the landing.

But the real key behind effective training is *cross-training*—a method
of practicing, conditioning, or working out that does not directly

involve the specific sport an athlete specializes in. For example, a track athlete might do some cycling work as a method of cross-training. Cross-training activities are not meant to replace the training schedule. Instead, cross-training acts as a sport enhancer, building muscle strength, coordination, balance, quickness, and explosiveness.

When developing a cross-training schedule for your child, you and your child's coach should tailor the workouts towards your child and his skills that need improvement. For example:

- *Off-court training* is important for tennis and basketball athletes. A tennis player might need agility training for reaching the ball and strength training to improve stroking power and muscle endurance.
- *Dry-land training* is helpful for swimmers because it allows them to improve the muscle strength of their upper back and back of the shoulders, which are not specifically strengthened while swimming. Activities could include weight training, running, biking, or jump training.
- *Off-ice training* is healthy for hockey players and figure skaters. This includes weight training, biking, jump training, and agility training. (See Chapter Thirteen: Flexibility, Strength, and Conditioning for more agility drills.)

NUTRITION FOR THE ELITE ATHLETE

Elite athletes need more calories than the average athlete, especially those elite athletes who train in endurance sports. This is to help meet the demands of their sport, as well as to grow. An adolescent in his or her growth spurt (ages twelve to fifteen for boys, ages nine to twelve for girls) may need 2,500 to 3,000 calories a day. Elite athletes who train twelve or more hours a week may need as many as 3,000 to 5,000 calories a day. Some children, especially those involved in strength sports such as football and lacrosse, may need a greater intake of protein. Foods that are high in protein include chicken, turkey, lean meat, and fish. This additional protein helps build extra muscle that's needed for the sport.

It is equally important for the young elite athlete to eat proper meals and snacks before, during, and after the game. The pregame meal should be eaten one to three hours before competition, while the postgame meal should be eaten a half-hour to two hours after. A few guidelines to remember:

- If your child doesn't ingest enough food before a match, or if his pregame meal is too early (more than three hours beforehand) his energy stores become depleted and his muscles won't function to their fullest. The result: Your child will fatigue early. This will have a negative effect on the current competition or practice session, as well as the next.
- If your child's pregame meal is too soon before a match (less than an hour beforehand), his body won't have time to digest the meal. The result: Your child may become nauseous and might vomit during the game.
- During competition, it is best to eat small meals and healthy snacks to keep going strong.

Athletes must keep hydrating themselves before, during, and after sporting events. If the athlete is dehydrated, the muscles don't work and the youngster can't compete or practice at her best. Athletes should also avoid drinking caffeinated drinks. Kids may take caffeine because they believe it will boost their performance, but in reality caffeine dehydrates the body and often makes athletes jittery.

Another good technique for athletes who want to examine their diet and performance is keeping a Three-Day Dietary Recall—an analysis of everything the athlete has had to eat and drink during a three-day period. The accumulated information will show your child's total consumed calories and how many of these calories are from carbohydrates, proteins, and fats. It is important to remember, elite athletes need more calories than other athletes and non-athletes, and some need more protein, depending on the sport. This is all necessary to make sure the caloric intake is adequate for rigorous activity and for child growth. The Three-Day Dietary Recall should be done once a year. It should be evaluated by a doctor or a nutritionist who has a good knowledge of sports nutrition. (See Chapter Fourteen for an example of a Three-Day Dietary Recall.)

Female athletes, especially those involved in endurance sports such as track, swimming, and cycling, often suffer from a high degree of iron deficiencies. This may adversely affect their sports performance. It is critical for these females to eat foods high in iron, such as green leafy vegetables, red meat, or dried fruits. (See Chapter Five for additional information on the special needs of the female athlete, and see Chapter Fourteen for additional information on nutrition.)

SLEEP AND REST FOR THE ELITE ATHLETE

All kids to need to grow and recharge their energy, and this happens while they sleep. But the elite child athlete needs even more sleep than the average kid. Sleep allows these children to recover from their workouts. Without enough sleep, their muscles become more sore and tired because the body does not have enough fuel to recharge itself. Adequate sleep guards against mental fatigue and keeps the mind fresh. This is necessary for strategy and communication, two important aspects of competitive sports. Adequate sleep also helps these very busy children keep up with their other responsibilities, such as homework and household chores. I recommend a minimum of eight hours of sleep a night. When a big competition is ahead, nine or ten hours of sleep is great. Sometimes a one-hour nap during the day can help refresh a youngster.

I also recommend that your child takes a week off from training every two to three months to prevent burnout, injuries, and to keep his interest in the sport fresh. The kids who get injured the most are those who do not take this time off. If it's not possible to take any time off, perhaps your child can have a lighter workout instead during the recommended rest period.

INJURIES AND THE ELITE ATHLETE

At some point throughout each year, it is inevitable that a serious athlete will suffer some type of injury. If your injured child continues to play, a more severe injury will result. Keep in mind that it is better to miss one tournament than to miss an entire season, so be aware of the early warning signs of injury. Sports doctors classify injuries into two distinct types: acute injuries and overuse injuries.

Acute injuries happen at a specific time and place. Some acute injuries are preventable, and those that are not are due to unforeseen circumstances. Acute injuries can be prevented by:

- *Making sure the playing field is in good shape.* For example, there should be no divets on lacrosse or soccer fields and no water on a basketball court.
- *Strictly enforcing the rules of the game.* Sports officials should oversee the players to ensure that the rules are followed and that no unnecessary rough play occurs, especially in football, hockey, and lacrosse.
- *Wearing protective equipment.* For example, wear shin guards in soccer and knee and shoulder pads in football.

Overuse injuries occur from repetitive use of the same muscles in motion. Repetitive use causes stress on these muscles, without enough time for recovery. The result is excessive inflammation, pain, and finally injury. The majority of overuse injuries are preventable, but there are two factors that lead to overuse injury. They are intrinsic and extrinsic.

Extrinsic Factors

Extrinsic factors are those factors related to the sport. They include:

1) *Training mistakes.* Common training mistakes are working too much, too soon, too fast. This is the most common cause of overuse injury. For example, increasing one's running distance from five to ten miles at one time.
2) *Equipment mistakes.* Using poor fitting equipment or equipment that is old is setting your child up for injury.
3) *Environment.* Consider whether it's too hot or too cold when your child is playing. When it's too cold, the muscles are stiff and injure easily; if it's too warm, the muscles are prone to dehydration, which can lead to injuries.
4) *Hydration status.* If your child is dehydrated, her muscles will fatigue more easily and this will lead to injury.
5) *Nutritional factors.* As we discussed earlier, if a kid enters practice or a competition without eating, the muscle energy stores will be low, and your athlete will fatigue more easily and get injured.
6) *Playing surface.* Kids training on concrete versus grass or other soft surfaces will more likely suffer from ankle, shin, or knee pain.

Intrinsic Factors

Intrinsic factors are physical traits, unique to the individual athlete.

1) *Anatomic misalignment.* For example, having high arched feet, being bowlegged or having knocked knees may predispose your child to injury. Parents should purchase sneakers with good arch support and well-cushioned heels. Shoe inserts or over-the-counter orthotics may prove useful.
2) *Muscle imbalance.* Overdeveloped muscles in the front of the shoulder paired with weak muscles in the back of the

shoulder can lead to injuries. Parents of elite swimmers, baseball pitchers, and tennis players should help their youngsters do resistance training to improve upper back and shoulder strength. (See Chapter Thirteen: Flexibility, Strength, and Conditioning for more information.)

3) *Deconditioned body*. The warning goes, "Out of season, out of shape." Slacking off on an exercise routine between seasons can lead to injuries, so all athletes should make an effort to remain active, even off-season.

4) *Prior injury*. For example, shin splints or shoulder tendonitis can easily flare up again.

Tips For Elite Athletes and Their Parents

- Don't play through pain.
- Once you've been injured, take time to heal—ignoring an injury will only make it worse.
- Wear proper size protective equipment and maintain safe playing conditions.
- Recognize the early signs of an overuse injury, such as inflammation and pain.
- Rehabilitate all injuries, both minor and severe.
- Don't return your child to competition unless he has regained full strength and range of motion.
- Communicate the severity of the injury to the coach, so proper attention can be given to the injury.

MENTAL TOUGHNESS

What separates a good athlete from an elite athlete is mental toughness. Often in an individual sport, the athlete with the greater mental strength will prevail over the most gifted athlete. Lance Armstrong won the 1999, 2000, and 2001 Tour de France bike races after he was diagnosed with testicular cancer. His story represents the following qualities:

- Self-confidence
- Perseverance
- Motivation
- The ability to respond well to adversity
- Always wanting to improve one's performance
- Concentration
- Having the "competitive edge" or "killer instinct"

These are all qualities that help an elite athlete rise to the top. Often champions are born with these qualities. With practice and success in competition, an elite athlete may continue to improve her mental strength.

THE COACH

Along with the parents and the athlete himself, the coach plays a critical role in the success of the elite child athlete. A good coach often takes on the role of trainer, sports psychologist, and nutritionist. This coach should be encouraging and should tell your child to never give up. He also knows when to have your child's injury evaluated. And when your young athlete is training too hard or not enough, the coach will know. Most importantly, look for a supportive coach, not one who is punitive.

Qualities of a Good Coach

- Energetic
- Supportive
- Enthusiastic
- Knowledgeable about the sport and practice drills
- Nice to kids
- Encouraging to all, not just the star
- Fair and equal treatment for all players
- Able to teach discipline and sportsmanship

Warning Signs of a Bad Coach

- Too critical
- Overly controlling
- Withholds fluid and food from youngsters
- Plays favorites
- Displays a bad temper
- Doesn't know the rules of the game or drills
- Sore loser

THE YEARLY TUNE-UP

Having a yearly fitness profile is critical to optimize the athletic performance of your youngster. A fitness profile is a series of tests and analyses of your child's physical and emotional strengths and weaknesses. It allows the athlete, along with the coach, to design and enhance an appropriate training program. It may be performed by a group of health care professionals such as a physician, nutritionist, physical therapist, and sports psychologist. The fitness profile includes:

- *Sports physical.* This should be done to screen for any medical conditions that may hamper sports performance, such as exercise-induced asthma or problems with the heat.
- *Muscle strength testing, also called Isokinetic testing.* I also recommend Isokinetic testing of shoulders and knees to test for any muscle weakness or muscle imbalance. The dominant side should be no more than 10 percent to 15 percent stronger. A muscle strength difference of more than 15 percent to 20 percent would indicate injury susceptibility on that side.
- *Muscle flexibility testing.* The upper body (shoulders) and lower body (hamstrings and quadriceps) should be assessed

to see if there is any tightness that predisposes to injury and suboptimal performance.

- *Three-Day Dietary Recall.* This is necessary to determine whether the athlete is taking in enough calories and the proper amount of nutrients. Should also include a pre- and postgame nutrition analysis. (See Chapter Fourteen for an example of a Three-Day Dietary Recall.)
- *Sports psychology review.* This will assess the athlete's self-esteem, communication skills, and ability to maintain confidence and the competitive edge.
- *Review of any injuries and treatments in the past year.*
- *Analysis of any injury patterns to show weak muscle groups or reveal any over-training.*

In addition, your child and the doctor should look toward the future, reviewing past accomplishments and setting upcoming goals. They should examine:

- Strengths and weakness of athletic skills
- Yearly goals
- Yearly accomplishments (personal best)
- Career goals in sport

PROS AND CONS OF THE ELITE CHILD ATHLETE

The Positives

Being an elite young athlete has many positive aspects. These include learning leadership qualities, enhancing self-esteem, dealing with adversity, gaining motivation, earning a possible college scholarship, learning time management skills, attaining superior physical health, and having a good body image.

The Negatives

Many young athletes face enormous pressures, both from those around them and from themselves. When a young athlete trains for too many hours or follows too intense a regimen, a complex known as the "over-training syndrome" can occur. This is characterized by a decrease in athletic performance, mental and physical fatigue, irritability, short temper, and personality changes. Other negatives include burnout, depression, stress, lack of sleep, playing with pain, and suffering frequent injuries.

STRESS MANAGEMENT

It's important for your child to look at her involvement with her sport as fun. If she views it as work, she is at risk for early burnout. Of course there might be days when their sport is not enjoyable, but that is a common emotion.

Tips for the Parents of an Elite Athlete

- Don't encourage your child to play through pain.
- Look for a supportive coach.
- Insist that your child wears proper equipment.
- Keep your child's workouts interesting.
- Make sure your young athlete has one or two days off a week from training.
- Arrange for your child to have one to two consecutive weeks off every three months.
- Let your elite athlete have as normal a childhood as possible.
- Have family time that is not related to your child's sport.
- Know when to help your child train harder or when to back off.
- Know when to bring your youngster to the doctor.

- Keep an eye out for signs of iron and calcium deficiency in young female athletes. Fatigue and poor concentration may indicate iron deficiency. Fractures that take longer than expected to heal or multiple stress fractures may indicate a calcium deficiency.
- Have good communication between your child's doctor, coach, trainer, and nutritionist.
- Make sure your youngster is getting adequate sleep and nutrition.
- Make sure your child is having fun.

Q&A WITH DR. SMALL

Q My twelve-year-old-daughter was a competitive gymnast heading for elite status. Unfortunately, she grew three inches in the last year, and her coach feels that she is now too tall to compete at her previous level. My daughter still loves the sport and competition, but I believe she needs to channel her energies into a new activity. Any suggestions?

A You are wise to consider alternatives. You may encourage your daughter to continue with gymnastics, but with the emphasis on fun rather than competitiveness. You may also encourage her to train in another sport, with an eye towards future competition, if that is what she's looking for. Many gymnasts do well in figure skating, or she might like track. With proper coaching, she should do well in whatever sport she selects.

Q My son is a running back in football, but recently I've noticed that he's become overly cautious with the ball. He's won a full athletic scholarship to a very good college. Should I be worried?

A Often an athlete may "choke" under pressure-filled situations. In these circumstances, it is best to have the athlete focus on some positive aspect of the game. This is called visualization. Also, repetitive practice situations are useful because they simulate real game situations.

Q Is it possible to peak too early in a sport?

A It is possible to peak at an early age and not get any better. With good coaching, one can hope that your child can continue to improve his athletic skills and strategy.

Q My daughter has a badly sprained ankle and has a tournament next week. There will be many college coaches scouting the kids. Should I allow my daughter to participate?

A If she is able to run, jump, and shoot at 90 percent of her capability, then I would permit her to play. I would suggest supportive taping or bracing to provide the ankle with extra support. You should remind her, however, to stop playing if she feels worsening pain. It would also be a good idea for her to play fewer minutes at a time than she usually does.

Q My fourteen-year-old daughter runs track year-round. She's had a number of injuries in the past six months—shin splints, runner's knee, and several ankle sprains. Is she injury-prone, or is she training incorrectly?

A This is a complicated question to answer. Your daughter's problem may be a combination of factors. She may be running too much. She may have had a growth spurt recently and her muscles may have tightened up, predisposing her to injury. But this series of injuries are definitely not just a "normal" part of running. It's time for your daughter to visit a doctor who specializes in sports and children; perhaps a new combination of training, nutrition, and rehabilitation is necessary. Finally, you and your daughter's doctor should also investigate her nutrition and menstrual status; she may be suffering from the female athlete triad. (See Chapter Five for more information.)

Q My son runs fifty miles a week in preparation for an important national meet. Do you think this is too much?

A Fifty miles a week may or may not be too much—it depends upon how far he was running the previous few weeks. He should not increase his distance more than 10 percent in any week. If he is increasing his distance too much too fast, he might injure himself and miss his meet.

Q My daughter is a national-level figure skater. She has a stress fracture in the lower back (spondylolysis). Her physician says she has to give up figure skating. Is this so?

A Your daughter does not have to give up figure skating. The most important thing is to get her fracture to heal. This is best achieved by doing physical therapy to strengthen abdominal muscles and improve hamstring flexibility, and by wearing a back brace twenty-three hours per day for three to nine months. The back brace is a custom-made brace that prevents excessive spine motion and promotes healing of the fracture. It is removed for showering and for doing physical therapy exercises. She may return to skating as soon as her pain goes away with hyperextension. Pain generally vanishes within one month of a good physical therapy program along with using the back brace.

Lower back stress fractures may occur in various sports. No matter what the sport, the same treatment holds true: physical therapy, back brace, and a gradual return to sports as the pain disappears.

Q My *fifteen-year-old son is an elite basketball player. He wants to take the month of August off. I think that this is important practice time. What do you think?*

A It looks like a compromise might be in order. Maybe he can take several weeks off instead of the whole month. I think it is good to take some time off, and when he returns to the sport he will more likely be rested, refreshed, and eager to start training hard once again. If your son doesn't take any time off, he will be frustrated and probably angry with you; he also may be distracted and wishing he were somewhere else instead of on the basketball court. He is growing up, and you need to give him a chance to contribute to the decision-making process.

CHAPTER FIVE

THE YOUNG, FEMALE ATHLETE

Kaitlyn, a shy, reserved, and somewhat insecure twelve-year-old girl, had never remotely thought of herself as athletic. Yet, she and her mother paid me a visit in June for a sports physical. Kaitlyn told me that she was thinking about joining the town soccer league in the fall. Her mother was concerned because her daughter had never played competitive team sports before, and from her reading on the subject, she worried that Kaitlyn could be susceptible to a sports injury. I asked Kaitlyn two simple questions:

1. *Among the girls in her class, where did she think she would finish in a sprint?*
2. *Where would she finish in a one-mile run?*

She answered, "Oh, probably last or near last" to both questions. With this background in mind, I made several recommendations:

A) *Kaitlyn should attend one of the several soccer clinics held yearly by her town that summer.*
B) *She should also cross-train with a parent or with her friends by running, jogging, or cycling at least three times a week. This preparation should include twenty minutes of continuous activity, such as aerobic training, along with her training for soccer.*

C) *She should learn the appropriate way to approach a workout. This workout should include:*

- *Aerobic Warm-Up—five to ten minutes of jogging, walking briskly, jumping rope, or doing jumping jacks.*
- *Flexibility Exercises—stretching of quadriceps, hamstrings, and calf muscles. Tip: Hold each stretch for twenty seconds and repeat two times for a total of six stretches. (See pages 165 and 178 for exercises.)*
- *Begin soccer practice routine.*

D) *She should keep a logbook of her training routine, increasing the intensity of her activity weekly.*

Three months later, I received a phone call from Kaitlyn's mother, thanking me for the advice. Kaitlyn had, in fact, joined the town recreational league and was happily playing soccer. In the short period of time between the summer school months and the fall, Kaitlyn's lack of self-esteem dissipated and her self-confidence soared. Her amazed parents were convinced that her emotional growth was due to the athletic skills she acquired and the new friends she had made.

YOUNG FEMALE ATHLETES: THE BENEFITS

In a nutshell, there are many basic reasons why physical activity is vital for girls. They are:

- Improved self-esteem
- Improved muscle strength
- Improved flexibility
- Improved balance
- Improved bone density
- Better academic achievement

- Lower risk for heart disease, diabetes, and stroke
- Improved energy levels

Kaitlyn's story resonates because it clearly shows that success in athletics, even later in childhood, dramatically increases a child's self-esteem and confidence level. Sports can offer rewarding experiences that may have more far-reaching effects than the physical activity itself.

Regular active participation in physical activity acts as a deterrent to physical and mental illness and social problems, as well as preventing coronary heart disease, osteoporosis, and cancers in the future. Girls who participate in sports are less likely to have an unwanted teen pregnancy, abuse drugs and alcohol, or engage in violent behavior.

Physical activity and sports are important in the prevention of problems such as childhood obesity. And competence in sports leads to a positive body image, a higher sense of self-esteem, and increased self-confidence, all important traits for young women in today's society. Sports are an educational asset in girls' lives, too—research findings show that high school athletes achieve higher grades, have lower dropout rates, and are more likely to go on to college than their non-athletic counterparts.

A study by the National Collegiate Athletic Association found that women student-athletes graduate at a significantly higher rate than women students in general. Participation in sports promotes the learning of social skills such as assertiveness, communication, and leadership. It is interesting to note that 80 percent of women identified as key leaders in Fortune 500 companies participated in sports during their childhood and self-identified as having been "tomboys."

In the past few years, research reports from the Centers for Disease Control, the Office of the Surgeon General, the Department of Health and Human Services, the President's Council on Physical Fitness and Sports, and the Women's Sports Foundation have all documented the benefits of physical activity and sports for girls. These same studies show that women with experience in sports are able to confront challenges and face critical situations throughout life with more confidence. Athletic activity also instills the skills of teamwork and a sense of camaraderie. It fosters a young girl's ability to define her individual goals, as well as her team goals.

We cannot overlook the impact on society, and especially among young girls, of female competitors in team sports. Over the past several years, a number of female role models have emerged in sports: Mia Hamm, Chamique Holdsclaw, Dominique Dawes. All one has to do is consider the U.S. Women's Soccer Team—after their World Cup soccer triumph in 1999, they appeared worldwide, exuding energy, confidence, and well-being. They truly epitomize the value of physical activity for young girls. Girls now know that becoming active in sports does not mean one must be "less than feminine." They are learning that increased stamina, emotional stability, and better physical health are the rewards of healthy physical activity.

Should coaches be providing advice to young female athletes regarding their weight? Girls should be concentrating on developing their skills, rather than their physicality. Well-meaning coaches and parents will often look at a girl's weight as an impediment to success in sports. Instead, these coaches should be focusing on reducing their specific weaknesses and enhancing their athletic strengths. A coach should not be advising a female athlete to lose weight in order to pick up speed, but instead should be working on drills that teach quickness and agility techniques. All girls can be athletic, no matter their size, shape, or weight.

The truth is that even though the differences between women and men's bodies are apparent, they respond to diet and training regimens in much the same way. Women who have learned the basics of all around good health—both physical and mental—include sports and athletic activity in their daily routine.

Such is the case for the majority of young women who do not play competitive sports or specialize in a singular athletic activity. It is now well known that exposure to proper exercise of any kind is key to mental and physical fitness throughout life. Aerobic exercise promotes heart and lung fitness, muscle strength, balance, personal accomplishment, a feeling of well-being and stress reduction—all factors that improve anyone's daily routine.

The important thing to remember is that physical activity of any type is not truly valuable or helpful unless it suits an individual's lifestyle. Not all girls or women are meant to swim. Certainly, not all are physiologically geared to run. It is critical for the families of young girls to encourage them to pursue activities that create enjoyment. Rollerblading may be the sport of choice, or basketball, or modern dance. As with all kids, it's important to help young women find activities that are healthy and fun, so they'll continue to reap the benefits of fitness and form habits that will last a lifetime.

YOUNG FEMALE ATHLETES: THE RISKS

Although there are many benefits that accompany regular physical activity, it is also important to be aware of the risks. Competition can sometimes place undue pressure and unrealistic expectations on young female athletes.

Take, for instance, the height/weight standard accepted by the American Medical Association. According to the Association's charts, a five-foot-tall woman should weigh no less than 100 pounds, and a five-foot-six-inch woman should weigh about 130 pounds. Yet a five-foot-six-inch-tall ballerina weighs on average around 110 pounds, approximately 20 percent lower in weight than normal.

An incident from recent history describes the result of such extreme weight loss. Twenty-two-year-old Olympic-caliber gymnast Christy Henrich had been bound for the 1992 Olympics in Barcelona.

In March of 1988 at a competition in Budapest, Hungary, she came within .118 of a point of making the Olympic trial cut-off. At the end of the competition, she approached a judge to find out how she could improve her scores. Without thinking about the consequences, he advised her to lose some weight. In the summer of 1994, her strict regimen of exercise and starvation caused her death, the result of massive organ failure caused by anorexia and starvation. The coroner's investigation found that the four-foot-ten-inch gymnast weighed slightly more than fifty pounds at her death.

The Female Athlete Triad

Christy Henrich is an extreme example of what can come from the "Female Athlete Triad." This expression was coined in 1992 by the American College of Sports Medicine, and girls who suffer from the Female Athlete Triad are described as exhibiting the following three characteristics:

- Disordered eating (intentionally skipping meals, starving, or bingeing and purging)
- Osteopenia (low bone density due to lack of proper nutrients)
- Amenorrhea (absence of menstrual periods)

Girls who are involved in *aesthetic sports*, such as ballet, gymnastics, figure skating, and diving are especially prone to the Female Athlete Triad. Those who participate in *weight-class sports*, such as karate, judo, crew, and *endurance sports*, such as long distance running, skiing, and cycling, are also susceptible.

Those who participate in weight-class sports may try to lose weight in an effort to compete at a lower weight class. Sometimes in the process of losing weight, they lose muscle mass as well, thereby decreasing their performance. In endurance sports, girls may be told to lose five or ten pounds to run more quickly, but this can backfire and hamper their performance. Again, with dramatic weight reduction, muscle is lost. Without the body's muscular support system, speed and endurance are lost as well. Regardless of the sport, at least one or more parts of the Female Athlete Triad may be seen in a high percentage of young female athletes. There is a great emphasis on young athletes to win—at all costs. Such pressure may lead to disordered eating and unnecessary attempts to lose weight. Parents and coaches must be sensitive about what they say regarding nutrition and body weight to young female athletes.

Disordered Eating

- "You eat like an horse."
- "If you keep eating that much, you'll end up looking like a cow."
- "Don't be such a pig."

All it takes to create an eating disorder is one of these phrases aimed at a particularly vulnerable young female athlete. Sadly, many young women who suffer from eating disorders simply never learned the basics of good nutrition. A recent study in the journal *Pediatrics* stated that unlike their female counterparts of a half-century ago, 99 percent of children age three to seventeen do not eat regular, well-balanced meals. Once susceptible children receive a trigger suggestion, such as the ones above, they can begin to skip meals or intentionally avoid foods with fat in them.

A typical meal for someone who is overanxious about weight control might be:

BREAKFAST:	A plain bagel with jelly and a cup of black coffee
LUNCH:	Tossed salad (without dressing), alfalfa sprouts, and black coffee
DINNER:	Low-fat yogurt and a bagel with twelve ounces of water

Although the foods mentioned are not unhealthy in themselves, they constitute in total only 600 calories! An adolescent girl requires no less than 1,500 to 2,000 calories a day simply to maintain weight to ensure proper growth and development. A young woman who intensely trains for a sport may require 3,500 calories or more.

In addition, the young woman who is eating the 600-calorie-a-day diet is lacking many important vitamins and minerals—most importantly, calcium and iron. Without calcium, active teenagers cannot achieve peak bone density, which places them at high risk for stress and acute fractures of the legs and feet. They are also likely to have more frequent injuries and take longer to recover. Without adequate iron intake, a young girl is likely to suffer from iron deficiency anemia. This condition results in poor attention span, muscle fatigue, and impaired performance.

The same young woman may also be taking laxatives or diuretics to lose weight. When used in this manner, these products can cause a severe electrolyte imbalance and a loss of the vital mineral potassium. Electrolyte imbalance leads to fainting, muscle instability, cardiac arrhythmias, and even death.

At the first sign of an eating disorder, parents should seek advice and help from the child's pediatrician and possibly a nutritionist. Eating disorders are more successfully treated when they are recognized and treated early. Warning signs that your child might have an eating disorder include:

- Rapid weight loss
- Eating alone
- Vomiting after meals or throughout the day
- Skipping meals
- Being secretive around meal times
- Refusing to eat in public places

Low Bone Density (Osteopenia)

Although the fastest growing population in sports is the young, female athlete, studies show that the young women involved in regular athletic activity incur injury at a three-to-five-time greater rate than young athletic males. This is sometimes attributed to declining bone density in the young women. Traditionally one thinks of low bone density (osteoporosis) as a disease of older, postmenopausal women, low bone density is being seen with increasing frequency in young girls, especially those who participate in aesthetic sports, weight class, and endurance events. When this is seen in young women, it is called *osteopenia*.

Many young female athletes hear "Play through it" from their coaches when they complain of pain. Many of these young athletes are told to rest for a week or so, but the pain usually returns. When a physician finally sees the athlete, he will prescribe rest. Some doctors may take an X ray and discover a stress fracture (an inflammation and weakening of the outer surface of the bone). Stress fractures, especially those that are recurring or those that take a long time to heal, are caused by osteopenia and too intensive of a training program without sufficient time of bone recovery.

If the doctor is mindful of the Female Athlete Triad, he will test for bone density, inquire about the young woman's menstrual history and eating habits, and give sound nutritional advice.

Lack of Menstrual Periods (Amenorrhea)

As mentioned above, *amenorrhea* (lack of menstrual periods) is a significant sign of disordered eating and hormone irregularity in young female athletes. There are two distinct types of amenorrhea—primary and secondary. Amenorrhea is considered primary when there are no menstrual periods with signs of puberty (breast development and pubic hair) by the age of sixteen. Secondary amenorrhea is defined when an adolescent girl misses three or more consecutive periods after she has already begun menstruating.

Both primary and secondary amenorrhea are fairly commonplace among elite female athletes. The major problem with prolonged amenorrhea of either type is that it leads to abnormally low bone density.

What is most problematic is that during these formative years, ages sixteen to eighteen, peak bone density is acquired. This is the amount of bone density that carries a woman through her adult years—and into old age. When a woman starts out with less bone density, she becomes much more susceptible to the effects of osteoporosis as her estrogen and progesterone levels drop and she enters menopause.

The aim of a physician working with a young woman suffering from amenorrhea is to return her adolescent body to proper hormonal levels and to allow for menstruation to begin again and bone density to develop at proper levels. To accomplish this, the young woman must increase her caloric intake, cut back on the number of hours of training per week, and even reduce the intensity of her training.

Without proper nutrition, enough rest, and appropriate exercise to prepare for the sport or athletic event, even the most talented young woman can compromise her health and reduce her potential.

The most common cause of injury to anyone who competes in sports or begins a new exercise program is doing too much, too soon, too fast. When one starts training at a high level, the body needs crucial time to recover and increase aerobic fitness, endurance, and muscle strength. If one ignores the body's signals, such as pain, then physical injury will result and fitness will not be achieved.

Such was the case with Lisa, a long distance runner. At age fifteen, Lisa had sustained a stress fracture of the second metatarsal bone in her right foot. The injury took eight weeks to heal, whereas normally such an injury should take only two to four weeks of recovery. But Lisa's bone density was so low and her nutritional habits so poor that the healing process took much more time than it should have.

Several months before the injury, Lisa had been advised by her coach to lose five pounds. As in the case of many females who get caught up in the Female Athlete Triad, Lisa doubled the amount that she was told to lose and dropped more than ten pounds in six weeks. The original stress fracture probably came as a result of poor nutrition and overtraining, but no one recognized the correlation at that time.

When she was seventeen years old, Lisa came to see me about a new pain in her foot. During her first visit to my office, I gave her a complete physical. X rays revealed that Lisa had a tibia stress fracture that required rest and then a gradual increase of low-impact activities. While we talked, she revealed that she hadn't had a menstrual period for eighteen months. This crucial bit of information helped me to understand that she suffered from Female Athlete Triad and why she was so susceptible to injury.

I advised Lisa to see a nutritionist, and she did so immediately. With this support (she added two small nutritious snacks a day, along with a calcium supplement) and continued monitoring, all of her injuries have healed. She has also gained back five pounds and says she hasn't felt this well in three years. Though she still has not recovered her menstrual periods, she remains on a nutritious diet and maintains a proper exercise program.

During the time that I was regularly seeing Lisa, I also referred her to a sports psychologist who works on self-esteem and body image issues. Fortunately, the multidisciplinary approach we used to make Lisa healthy again has had an enduring effect. The last time I heard from her, she told me that she routinely breaks school track records. That makes everyone involved with Lisa's care—especially Lisa— quite happy.

Q&A WITH DR. SMALL

Q *Are there sports that are better suited to girls, rather than boys?*

A Although there is certainly no sport from which a girl or a boy should be excluded, there are specific sports in which flexibility is key. In terms of physical composition, flexibility is a strong suit for girls and young women. They often excel in sports such as figure skating, dance, and gymnastics because their muscles, joints, and tendons are genetically developed to be more flexible. However, this flexibility may also predispose them to specific injuries, such as tearing of the anterior cruciate ligament of the knee (the major structure that reinforces and stabilizes the knee), patella femoral pain syndrome (pain and irritation in and around the kneecap known as "runner's knee"), recurrent ankle sprains, and chronic shoulder injury.

Q*Do all girls need to wear supportive bras while exercising?*

A Absolutely. When girls perform sports that require running or jumping, there can be considerable irritation to the breast tissue that can lead to redness, swelling, and even bleeding. Protection of all body areas that are likely to be irritated by motion should be protected.

Q*My teenage daughter has never been athletic and would like to get started. Do you have any suggestions?*

A Allow your child to choose a physical activity that interests her. Is your child introverted or social? Does she like group or individual activities? Introductory sports for a child who wants to be part of a team could be basketball or soccer. Leagues for these sports tend to encourage children of all sizes and aptitudes.

If your child wants to perform an individual sport, then golf, swimming, running, cycling, or simply walking are all good aerobic activities. Karate and recreational dancing are individual, noncompetitive activities that will serve the same purpose.

Q*My daughter complains about her body shape and figure all the time. I am afraid that she is developing a poor self-image, despite my encouragement, and I fear that she may try to reduce her weight and change her body shape with anorectic or bulimic means. What should I do?*

A It is good that you are so aware of your daughter's response to possible poor self-image, and you obviously supply ample comfort and motivation. You are on the right track, and to remain there, continue to build her self-esteem with positive reinforcement and continuous dialogue. Children who know they are being heard have a much greater advantage than those who believe there is no one out there to listen. However, please keep a vigilant eye, as she may be on the cusp of developing an eating disorder. In this case, a meeting with a social worker, psychologist, a physician, a nutritionist, or even an adult friend is in order.

Q *Should my twelve-year-old daughter be taking calcium supplements?*

A My answer may surprise you: preferably, no. I always try to encourage young women to obtain their calcium from food as opposed to supplements, since calcium from food is better absorbed. And a doctor who immediately recommends a pill or supplement sends the wrong message that all problems can be solved by taking a pill.

Yet, I have to qualify that answer with the fact that the majority of American females—young or old—do not get enough calcium in their daily diets. At all stages of their lives, women should be eating foods rich in calcium, such as low-fat milk, cheese and yogurt, and orange juice that is calcium-fortified as well as green leafy vegetables.

Keep in mind that peak bone density is achieved between the ages of sixteen and eighteen, and proper nutrition (including adequate calcium) is most vital at this time of life. If you are truly concerned that your child is not getting enough calcium because you believe her diet is not balanced, certainly consider adding supplements, but check with a physician or nutritionist as to how much and which type of calcium is best.

Q *My thirteen-year-old daughter is a nationally ranked tennis player. Just recently she seems to have tired of working so hard at her sport, to the extent that she wants to quit tennis entirely. Now she's more interested in cultivating an active social life, including parties at the homes of her friends almost every weekend. How can I explain to her that tennis and other athletic activities can be balanced along with a social life, without turning her off all sports completely?*

A It is true that girls drop out of sports at a rate six times higher than boys. It is important, therefore, to find the right motivators to enhance the sports experience for girls, whether or not they are top-notch players like your daughter.

I recommend that you encourage your daughter to remain active in tennis, although not on the same level at which she currently competes. I surmise that she has been practicing for at least four hours most days of the week and entering regular tournaments on the tennis circuit. I suggest that you encourage her to practice only one or two days a week, and encourage her to compete only in tournaments of her choice, three or four times a year. The reduction of activity will not reduce her tennis skills, only ease the stress that the elite athlete sometimes encounters. By allowing your daughter to self-regulate the number of hours of training, she will avoid the common phenomenon of "burnout." (For more information, see Chapter Four: The Elite Athlete.)

Please encourage your daughter to continue with tennis while she focuses on balancing her life. In this way, you provide the stepping-stones for her to take the successful path to adulthood.

Q My twelve-year-old daughter is not a superstar athlete; she plays on school sports teams for pure enjoyment. The problem is that her coaches don't encourage and support her for her effort and participation—their time and attention is given to the gifted athletes who really excel on the school teams. It annoys me that she's overlooked because she's not a top performer. What should I do to bring attention to this problem?

A Because of the current emphasis on superstar athletes, certain college sports, such as football and men's basketball, are seen as the "farm leagues" of professional sports rather than being viewed as one component of a solid college education. The stars of these sports receive large scholarships and other perks, and, in exchange, they are expected to practice and play without regard to their own health and welfare. It is expected that some of these athletes will go on to earn fortunes for themselves as well as for the owners of professional football and basketball teams. It's a lot of pressure for these elite athletes, and a lot of pressure, too, for the athletes who are not competing at this elite level of play. The reality is that most girls and boys will not be playing professional sports.

Parents and coaches should put an emphasis on "lifetime" sports in which everyone can participate. Walking, jogging, swimming, golf, tennis, cross-country skiing, biking, hiking, and horseback riding are fitness activities that people of all ages can enjoy, with little risk of injury.

Intramural sports, when properly supervised, can provide opportunities for exercise, fun, and teamwork for almost everyone. I think it's time for you to remind your daughter's coaches of this fact, for their sakes as well as your daughter's. You should have a private conversation with the coach regarding your concerns. You may want to try phrasing this as a question: How can my child help improve her skills? This way no one is accusing the coach of wrongdoing, but rather you are addressing the situation in a proactive manner.

Q *My sixteen-year-old daughter is mildly overweight. She does not exercise, and she eats junk food when she's not home. I have not drawn her attention to what I think of her weight problem, but I want to do something now, before her weight and lack of physical activity get out of hand. How should I approach her without turning her into an anorexic or bulimic?*

A Your daughter is among the millions of young people who seem to be exercising less and eating more. You are very insightful to recognize that this pattern could cause her problems now, as well as later on in life. I suggest two commonsense approaches to this issue:

- *Plan an exercise program to suit your entire family.* Of course, individuals in your family may have interest in different physical activities, but there is usually one activity that one or more family members can agree to do and enjoy together. For some families, it's tennis; for others, it's running or walking; some prefer golf or biking. Whichever you and your family agree to do should become an enjoyable part of your lifestyle, not just another thing that adds hours to your already crowded schedule. Once you try this, your family may begin to look forward to this change of pace. Later on, you and the others may choose another activity to try together. In any case, it keeps all of you in tune with the family dynamics, while providing a healthy workout.

- *Try to work with your daughter to decrease her caloric intake in the following ways:*

  A. Be aware of the number of sugary soft drinks she consumes in a day, and try to halve the amount.
  B. Limit high-fat, high-calorie snacks to a few times per week or special occasions, instead of allowing her to eat them on a daily basis.
  C. Check for the hidden calories and fat content in condiments and salad dressings, and limit the amount used at meals.
  D. Try to prepare homemade meals instead of buying prepared foods that almost always have a high fat, sugar, or salt content.

It's important to follow these recommendations as a family, so that your daughter does not feel she is being singled out. But most of all, avoid comparisons of her body shape or weight with her friends, family members, or high profile people, such as television personalities or models. At all times, praise her for her most positive traits, talents, and qualities.

Q *Is it safe for girls to weight train or will it "bulk them up" and make them appear unfeminine?*

A With an appropriate weight-training workout (low weights and high repetitions), girls will not bulk up. The low-weight approach will tone muscles and enhance their strength. If very heavy weights are used, there is the possibility of putting on extra muscle weight, which may appear "bulky."

Weight training can often boost the self-esteem of girls, who can safely weight train along with their male counterparts. All people who work with weights must, however, follow the appropriate guidelines, which include proper technique under the supervision of a qualified adult, with low weights and high repetitions. (See Chapter Ten: Weight Training and the Young Athlete for more information.)

CHAPTER SIX

THE HYPERACTIVE CHILD

Ryan has Attention Deficit Hyperactivity Disorder (ADHD). With this in mind, his parents thought their son should be active and involved in structured activities, so they enrolled him in his local soccer league. When it was time to play, Ryan ran onto the field with his teammates and practiced with great enthusiasm. The oval-shaped field had been divided up into four different playing areas. Within minutes of entering the field with his team, Ryan had wandered into another group's play area, and began to trip and tackle the other players. It was obvious he was confused, and it took several minutes to catch up with Ryan and bring him back among his team. Within minutes, Ryan did it again.

I happened to be the coach for Ryan's team (my son was in the group), and I was watching his behavior with great interest and concern. I saw Ryan enjoying being part of the team, but his frustration and confusion was evident. I suggested to his parents that they pay close attention to him throughout the game and to help keep him in focus. By the end of the season, it was great to see his self-confidence grow and his concentration improve. He even scored a goal!

The term Attention Deficit Hyperactivity Disorder (ADHD) was officially identified in 1994. Until then, the condition was simply referred to as Attention Deficit Disorder because researchers had not yet fully recognized that the condition is multifaceted. A person with ADHD used to be described as having a short attention span and as being easily distracted. In actuality, distractibility and inattentiveness are not synonymous, and hyperactivity is not always in concert with the first two symptoms. ADHD is now broken into three characteristics: inattentiveness, impulsiveness, and hyperactivity.

This definition takes into account that some children have little or no trouble sitting still or containing their behavior, yet they may have difficulty remaining attentive. Others may be able to pay attention for a while, but they soon lose focus and become impulsive and act out. The last type is a combination of both, where characteristics of the first two types are intensified when combined. Remember, to help children with ADHD, building self-esteem is the most important part of the plan.

HOW DOES A HYPERACTIVE CHILD REMAIN ACTIVE IN SPORTS?

There is no reason why your child with ADHD cannot fully participate in some kind of sport. But a hyperactive child usually does not do well with a team-based sport unless that child has lots of adult supervision. This does not mean that they can never play a team sport. I believe that the key to keeping your child with ADHD physically active is to find a sport that has more individualized attention.

Activities such as martial arts and dance instruction are less competitive, yet allow a child to participate in a group environment. Remember that choosing the right coach is as important as choosing the activity. A good coach for an ADHD child must be patient, able to explain things clearly, and able to direct your child.

One-on-one activities would also be great choices for ADHD kids. You might try rollerblading, walking, biking, or skateboarding. These are sports you can do with your child to help keep him in focus.

If your child insists on participating in a group sport, look for smaller groups and a good coach, and be prepared to help out with your child. These practices should be simple and completed in a shorter time so your child doesn't lose interest. There should be a specific routine for each practice. Remember that structure and repetition are important. It is a good idea to assign the ADHD child a task such as setting up the cones or picking up the balls at the end of practice to help her maintain focus. After countless drills in training, everyone on the team, including the child with attention difficulties, knows what they are doing.

PSYCHOTROPIC DRUGS: LIFESAVER OR LIFE LIMITER?

As discussed earlier, there are specific criteria required to make the diagnosis of ADHD, but at this point there is no cure for it. Treatment, everyone agrees, involves more than just medication; behavior modification, supportive counseling, and daily, weekly, and monthly planning and scheduling are equally as important. Generally, medication is not the cure-all. We emphasize the importance of choosing sports and activities to boost concentration.

The decision to prescribe any medication to treat ADHD, such as Ritalin, Adderall, Wellbutrin, or Cylert, must be a group decision made by the physicians, therapists, family, and child. It is important for everyone involved to be familiar with the medications, how to give them, what their side effects are, and how they affect the child.

If you decide to try Ritalin or other drugs, your child should be closely monitored for an initial trial period of several weeks to observe the positive and negative effects of the drug's use. A key to management is that parents and teachers observe the child's behavior and report their findings to their physician, usually by questionnaire. A decision can then be made whether to change the dose or the medication entirely.

Once a child settles into the medication, monitoring should take place at least every three months. The majority of children receive benefits from the medication, although each child responds differently. A child with or without the diagnosis of ADHD should not be given medication specifically to improve sports performance; this would be unethical. In addition, medication should only be given if the child is significantly affected in school as well as outside the classroom.

QUIZ: IS THIS YOUR CHILD?

1. You are sitting with your family at the dinner table and having a conversation. Does your child watch an insect who is trying to get in through a closed window, ignoring the conversation entirely?
2. Your son is playing the position of outfielder in T-ball, and the batter hits a grounder aimed toward your child. Is your son too busy watching the ants crawling in and out of an anthill to see the ball coming?
3. When you take your child to look at a preschool for the fall, does your child run wildly from room to room, knocking things from the shelves?
4. When your child's teacher asks a question of the class, does your child begin jumping up and down, moving both arms all around, while blurting out an answer—any answer—without being called on by the teacher?
5. If your child is at a birthday party and everyone is playing soccer, does he wander off toward the exit and start opening and closing the door?

If you answered yes to any of these questions, your child may have inattentive, impulsive, and/or hyperactive behavior. It is time for you to seek a diagnosis, to listen to what your diagnostician tells you, and to consider all of the management options. When everyone works together on a situation of this magnitude, the probability for a good outcome increases significantly.

Q & A WITH DR. SMALL

Q *What kind of summer sports camp would you recommend for my hyperactive child? This will be his first camp experience, and he is eight years old.*

A I would not recommend an all-sport camp because it might be too competitive for your son. As I said before, hyperactive children often get frustrated in a competitive environment, and camp is supposed to be fun! If you do choose to go that route, it should be a mixture of different sports so your child does not have to focus for a long period of time on one activity and become frustrated. Look for a sports camp that emphasizes fun and is noncompetitive. Summer sports camp for kids can be a wonderful growth experience—if it is handled well and chosen carefully.

Q *My six-year-old son was recently diagnosed with ADHD. My husband and I are both very athletic and played on teams in high school and college. What is destined for our son regarding sports?*

A Generally, children with ADHD do not become super athletes. That level of playing requires intense concentration, which an ADHD kid simply does not have. Yet there are all degrees of ADHD, and whether your son has a severe or mild degree of the condition, there is an activity for him. Remember that team sports usually are not the best way to go. Your son might do best one-on-one with just a parent or in a smaller group sport. Do not compare yourself with your child. Simply take the time to see what activity your son would enjoy.

Q *My seven-year-old daughter with ADHD had quite a few bad experiences with soccer and T-ball. She will not sign up for these activities next year, and I'm not sorry about that. But she wants to be involved with sports. Can you suggest what to do and where to look?*

A Since she has already tried two team sports, I would certainly recommend individual activities, where she is one-on-one with an adult who not only serves as a trainer but also a mentor. Your child could be swimming with a private instructor or taking a martial arts class. These sports are noncompetitive and, when done one-on-one with an adult, can provide improved self-esteem and social skills.

You also might try an activity for yourself and your daughter. You can act as the coach and/or mentor. You can rollerblade together, go hiking, or try bike riding. The two of you would get fit together, as well as spending special time with each other. Plus, you would be able to help your child stay focused.

Q *My child is on Ritalin. How will it affect her sports performance?*

A Ritalin or other similar drugs will not make her throw the ball farther or more accurately. In other words, it will not improve her physical performance. It will, however, assist in focus and concentration skills, and only in that way will the drug help your child.

Q *My child has ADHD. How long should I expect him to concentrate while doing a sports activity?*

A There is not specific time frame. However, an average eight-year-old can concentrate for an hour to an hour and a half. An eight-year-old with ADHD may only be able to concentrate for fifteen to forty-five minutes. These are just ranges. You really have to know your child to see where he falls to make arrangements for an appropriate sports activity.

Q *Can I do anything at home to boost my son's sports concentration skills?*

A Yes—practice, practice, practice. Repetitive skill practice is very important in improving your son's concentration. But remember, don't practice so much that it ceases to be fun.

CHAPTER SEVEN

THE OVERWEIGHT CHILD

Justin, age nine, suddenly got chubby. His mom came to me to figure out why.

"He plays soccer and basketball twice a week, has gym twice a week, and has recess everyday," she said, "plus, I carefully watch what he eats." I asked if she really knew what else Justin was eating and suggested she ask her son what he ate while he was in school.

Justin was having lots of high-calorie snacks during the day. His class often had snacks with lots of calories and high fat content, such as sugared cookies and store-bought muffins. Justin also often bought his lunch and chose to eat only the snack portion, which consisted of candy. After school, Justin frequently went to various friends' homes and was almost always served chips or cookies as a snack.

And it turned out that Justin was not getting as much exercise as his mom thought. In his soccer games he played goalie, which involves little to no running. In basketball he only played several minutes each game, and the rest of the time he sat on the bench. He was not going out for recess everyday, so that was time with little physical activity, too. All these activities were not enough to make up for the extra calories Justin was eating.

After six months of encouragement and eight visits to my prescribed program (a nutritionist, an exercise professional, and me), Justin made remarkable changes. He embarked on a *walking program with his parents, thirty minutes two times a week. He was able to limit his high-fat, high-calorie snacks to two times per week, he cut his juice and soda intake in half, and he was eating smaller portion sizes. He had grown one inch, lost five pounds during this time period, and was very pleased with himself.*

OBESITY IN CHILDREN

Being overweight in today's society is "politically incorrect," and we are not likely to see a change in this perception. One only needs to glance at a man, woman, or child to unconsciously decide if the person is overweight, normal, or slender.

In the past twenty years, obesity among children ages six to eight has increased 54 percent! Another staggering fact is that anywhere from 20 to 30 percent of North American children are now overweight, which means 10 to 15 million American children deal with the problem of excess weight, perhaps throughout their entire lives. We need to take this issue seriously. Being overweight in youth can be the start of a lifetime of serious health problems.

There is a distinction between overweight and obesity. Obesity is defined as being more than 20 percent over ideal weight. For example, a child whose ideal weight is 100 pounds would be considered obese at 120 pounds. A child whose ideal weight is 50 pounds would be considered obese at 60 pounds. Your child's pediatrician can help you determine the range of ideal weight for your child, or you can obtain a copy of the National Standards for Height and Weight chart at your local library.

For every inch that a child grows they should gain 3 to 4 pounds. If a child grows two inches and stays the same weight, in effect, they have lost 6 to 8 pounds.

MEDICAL PROBLEMS ASSOCIATED WITH OBESITY

Overweight children are often short of breath, with or without exertion, and they are prone to asthma and exercise-induced asthma. Overweight children may also develop joint pains in their backs, knees, and ankles. More often than their smaller counterparts, they suffer from heat exhaustion, and worse still, low self-esteem.

Your child's pediatrician has no doubt been measuring your child's height and weight throughout the years. Children should generally be within the same percentile in height and weight (for example, fiftieth percentile for both height and weight, or seventy-fifth percentile for both height and weight). If the weight increases to the seventy-fifth percentile while the height remains at the fiftieth percentile, this might become a problem.

The weight-percentile figure is not always a sign of a child becoming overweight—there are many children who gain weight first and then go on to grow several inches a short time later. Growth spurts are often very uneven. But if it seems your child is becoming somewhat overweight, the solutions aren't simple. Weight control is a complex issue, requiring lifestyle changes and a concerted effort to live a healthier way of life. This includes proper exercise, sound nutrition, and an active lifestyle.

PROPER EXERCISE

Currently, 25 percent of children do not participate in any form of regular physical or family activity. A generation ago, children played in their backyards, in the street, and in playgrounds. They also had recess one or two times a day at school. Today, kids simply have a lunch break with no recess.

It's up to you to encourage your child to partake in physical activity, establishing habits now that will hopefully remain through adulthood. Some helpful hints for increasing activity for the whole family are:

- Use stairs instead of an elevator.
- Park in the back of the parking lot and walk the distance to the store, school, or office.
- If possible, encourage your kid to walk, bike, or rollerblade to school (remembering at all times to wear a helmet!).
- Have a year-round activity plan for your child's after-school activities. For example, soccer in the fall, indoor swimming in the winter, baseball or softball in the spring, and formalized camp program in the summer.
- Find noncompetitive activities that look like fun for your child. Martial arts, dance, and yoga are ideal for those kids who are just beginning to routinely exercise.
- Take frequent walks.
- Play in the park.
- Ride bikes.
- Swim (with supervision).
- Dance to music.
- Play tag.

Exercise should never be punitive in nature. Do *not* have a child run laps or do push-ups to punish her. And food should not be used as a reward, either—incentives and prizes for good behavior should be nonfood items, such as a fun family activity or buying a new piece of athletic equipment.

A fun and effective means to encourage physical activity would be to employ the FIT principle for the family. *F* stands for Frequency, *I* is for Intensity, and *T* is for Time. The family can monitor their progress of physical activity by keeping a calendar.

- *Frequency.* To begin with, setting aside one time a week for activity is sufficient. The goal at the end of six to nine months is for the family and the child to be exercising together three to four times a week.

- *Intensity*. Intensity is a harder concept to quantify. This tenet refers to how hard a person can exercise. We grade the intensity by mild, moderate, or severe. Mild refers to walking at a slow pace; severe exercise is at a level where a child is gasping for breath and sweating profusely. Moderate exercise is what we strive for.
- *Time*. Time refers to how many minutes of continuous exercise one can perform. The FIT principle is merely a concept and serves as a guideline for increasing one's level of physical activity.

If your child is struggling with his weight, choose sports that use weight to an advantage. Football and hockey are two sports that rely on weight. Swimming is another good activity; overweight kids are more buoyant than thinner kids, and they won't get cold as quickly. As a family, try enjoyable physical activities such as walking, biking, or skating. You are not necessarily looking to create a world-class athlete; you are looking to encourage lifelong leisure activity.

SOUND NUTRITION

Part of your role as a parent includes being a nutritionist, and a perfect way to start is to decrease fat and sugar intake for your family. The average kid needs to eat less fried food, drink less soda and sport drinks, and cut down on sweets and cookies.

Many families eat out three or more times a week and consume burgers, fries, hot dogs, pizza, and ice cream. Although it is OK to eat these foods once a week, if consumed on a daily basis they may contribute to your child becoming overweight.

Here are some ideas to help your child eat healthy, tasty balanced meals:

- Instead of drinking whole, one, or two percent milk, switch to skim.
- Breakfast cereals should be free of extra sugar, and eliminate extra syrup and butter on French toast, pancakes, and bread. Tasty alternatives include adding fresh fruit (strawberries or blueberries) to the top of pancakes—or even into the batter itself. My kids love banana pancakes, and they don't even know the fruit is already in there!
- Burgers, when made with turkey or lean red meat and broiled, are a healthy and excellent source of iron, B vitamins, and protein.
- French fries can be a good source of fiber—and a lot less fattening if prepared correctly. Try baking the potatoes instead of frying them, and this time brush the pan and the top of the fries with a small amount of olive oil. Sweet potatoes prepared in this manner are a good alternative and an even better source of vitamins. Health food stores offer a lower-fat version of french fries, and these might be worth investigating if you don't like to cook.
- Pizza is one of the healthier fast foods—the cheese contains calcium, and the tomato sauce has lycopene, an important nutrient for your health. Choose vegetable-topped pizzas, which are a good way to get added vitamins, and avoid high-fat meat toppings.
- Hot dogs, although fun to eat, are high in saturated fat and high in sodium. Limit how often your youngster eats a hot dog—only once or twice a month, perhaps weekly during the summer months.

Here are some other tips to keep your child's meals healthy:

- Don't deny dessert at every meal. Be careful, however, about the types of dessert you offer. A cup of low-fat or nonfat frozen yogurt can be as good as regular ice cream.
- Encourage your child to help you prepare meals, and talk with

her about the choices you make about food. Experts agree that this is a good way to encourage better eating habits.

- Encourage children to stay seated throughout the meal and talk with the family. Meals should be a social activity, not eaten in haste. Eating "on the run" makes overeating more likely since you're less likely to realize your stomach is full.
- For children under the age of ten, it's a good idea to use smaller serving plates to control portion size.
- Have lots of fruit and vegetables already cut up and ready to eat.
- Reduce juice intake by half, and dilute fruit juices with water. This reduces calories but still satisfies your child's thirst.
- Prepare a lower number of fried foods.
- Ensure that treats and snacks have some nutritional value. Steer away from foods with empty calories (soda, chips, candy).
- Don't let your child skip meals. A growing kid needs food every two to four hours to keep the mind and body functioning properly, and skipping meals tends to cause overeating at the next meal.
- Do not put your child on a "diet"—this singles him out and can cause embarrassment and resentment. The best solution is to quietly change the eating habits of your whole family.
- Don't be fooled by ads that say "no cholesterol" or "no fat"; these foods often contain lots of calories. It's always better to prepare simple, fresh meals when possible.
- Don't feed your child commercially prepared diet foods and low-fat shakes—they are not as fresh and are packed with preservatives. This food's very presence on a dinner table will single out the overweight child as "different."

ACTIVE LIFESTYLE

Let's talk about television for a moment. Youngsters are watching up to twenty-five hours of television per week. Programs geared toward kids are often full of advertisements for junk food, and kids tend to eat while they're watching TV. In addition, a child's heart rate is even lower while watching television than it is while reading a book. Take the low heart rate and the increased consumption of high-fat and high-sugar foods, and you have an ideal setup for weight gain. Television watching, computer games, and videos are all sedentary activities that need to be monitored and limited to a set number of hours per week.

Here are some tips:

- Limit television viewing and other sedentary activity to one hour per day (as recommended by the American Academy of Pediatrics).
- Discuss alternate activities with your child (inline skating or biking) rather than the sedentary ones. A parent can encourage doing fun things together or with a friend.
- Recommend outdoor activity on a daily basis.

SET AN EXAMPLE

The best thing a parent can do to help a child struggling with weight gain is to set a positive example. Tina, who was only eight years old and four feet tall, weighed over 180 pounds. After an evaluation of Tina's medical history and nutritional habits, I was able to estimate her caloric intake at more than 5,000 calories a day. Dinner often consisted of two hamburgers and french fries with sugary soda. She watched about five hours of television a day.

Her mother's own routine mirrored the child's. My staff and I were terribly bothered by Tina's hypertension, weight, morbid obesity, and lack of physical activity. We worked together to convince the mother that Tina needed immediate hospitalization, to which they agreed.

Tina stayed in the hospital for two months, and was given a 1,500-calorie diet and daily exercise sessions with trainers and physical therapists. During that time, she lost 35 pounds and began to feel better. Her mom, too, had picked up some healthy tips, and the two of them were able to motivate each other. In Tina's case, it took extreme measures to get on the road to a healthier lifestyle.

Q&A WITH DR. SMALL

Q My ten-year-old daughter is already being teased because she is slightly overweight. She is asking for low-calorie, high-protein shakes after seeing ads for them on television, and she wants to eat them for meals. Please tell me how to handle this.

A Obviously, your daughter is suffering from low self-esteem. Please compliment her on her positive attributes. If she absolutely wants to lose weight, she should do it in a safe way. Low-calorie, high protein shakes are not safe for children. These shakes may be too low in calories to support growth, and in addition, they lack important vitamins and minerals. Try limiting high fat and high calorie snacks in your daughter's diet, and be careful to control portion size. You should also be sure to make an effort to exercise together as a family.

Q My ten-year-old-son says that he's being teased all the time about being overweight and slow, even though he is very active in sports such as hockey and soccer. The kids call him "jelly belly." Do you have any recommendations for what we can do?

A There are some children, as well as some adults, who genetically have a certain appearance. For example, they may have thin arms and legs and a protuberant abdomen. If this is the case, you must teach your son how to deal with his body shape. He may, however, be overweight all over—arms, legs, and belly. In this case, you and your child's doctor can promote exercise, sound nutrition, and an active lifestyle to help change your son's body shape. It's also important to boost your child's overall self-esteem and to praise him about his other fine qualities that have nothing to do with weight. If significant teasing persists, it may be wise to seek counseling from a mental health professional (social worker, psychologist, or psychiatrist).

Q How long will it take for my child to lose weight?

A The real emphasis for you and your child should be on making lifestyle changes, not on the weight loss. However, most kids will need three to six months to see significant signs of weight loss. In order for the weight loss to be effective, it must be the result of small changes in one's habits. If you try to employ sweeping changes in your child's diet and exercise routine all at once, she will soon revert back to the same old habits.

Q Are there any side effects to rapid weight loss in children?

A Yes, there are many bad things that can happen. First, in addition to losing fat the child will also be losing muscle and bone. The child will likely have low energy and often become cranky and short-tempered. He can even become dehydrated and faint.

Q What burns more calories: exercising on a treadmill or on a stationary bicycle?

A If the exercise duration and intensity are the same, exercise on a treadmill will burn more calories. But I would not choose one over the other just because of the calorie difference. Your child will more than likely get bored with the treadmill or the stationary bike. I would suggest more fun activities—regular biking, rollerblading, or hiking.

Q Are there any sports my overweight child should avoid?

A If your child enjoys a certain sport, then I would encourage him to do that activity. Generally speaking, overweight children do not like to run; when your child is first starting an exercise routine, sports involving a great deal of running (soccer, basketball, lacrosse) are not my first recommendation.

Q My five-year-old boy is quite overweight. Are there any foods he should avoid?

A I would not necessarily tell your son to avoid foods. Instead, I would focus on portion size. Also, I would try to limit his treats to one per day initially. Many times, overweight children are eating three or four high-calorie treats per day. I would also monitor his juice and soda intake—an eight-ounce glass of orange juice has 120 calories, and a twelve-ounce glass of soda has 150 calories. Often decreasing this beverage intake in half, and supplementing it with water, is a good way to cut calories.

Dr. Small's Exercise and Nutrition Plan for the Overweight Child

A SIX-MONTH PROGRAM

Sometimes, the tips parents hear from their doctor about helping their child lose weight are not easy to implement. With this in mind, several other health care professionals and I have developed a multidisciplinary plan to support an overweight child and her family in their endeavor.

Our exercise and nutritional plan requires six monthly visits to the doctor's office, where each child and family member who attends is informed, supported, and encouraged to move forward to a healthy lifestyle. Here are the basic steps:

Visit One:

Child and parent meet with Dr. Small, a nutritionist, and an exercise specialist. During the hour-long visit, the family discusses its problems regarding weight control, its difficulties with regular activity, and other issues that may help or hinder their child's progress. During the session, the exercise specialist begins to work with the child to plan a fun and enjoyable workout. Later, the child and the family receive nutrition counseling, as well as activity goals and a chart to plot their progress. A sample activity goal might be a twenty-minute walk with a family member twice a week, or a weekly after-school dance class or martial arts class. We generally try not to give more than three goals at any one visit. We would rather the child accomplish one or two goals and feel good about it than giving him ten goals he cannot achieve.

Visit Two:

At this session, the child meets solely with the nutritionist and exercise specialist to measure results and reformat goals. There is ample praise for both the child and the parent for prior achievement and faithfulness to the program. The child again works out with the exercise professional for at least fifteen minutes to increase his enjoyment of physical movement and to add on more fun activities. We try to have the child work out with the exercise professional at each visit.

Visit Three:

This session is the same as visit two.

Visit Four:

At this juncture, I again meet with the child, the parent, nutritionist, and exercise professional to more closely monitor progress. I conduct a quick physical and very often see improved results.

Visit Five:

This visit is the same as visits two and three.

Visit Six:

This last session is a recap of all that has been discussed and tried. Our clients offer an evaluation of the program with recommendations on how it may be improved. The patients and families also tell us what worked best for them, and what was their favorite aspect of the program. These visits are monthly, but can be scheduled more frequently if needed. Many patients also begin an exercise program with a personal trainer. There are some insurance carriers who view this program as preventive, and in other cases, totally necessary if a child is morbidly obese.

CHAPTER EIGHT

THE UNNATURAL ATHLETE

Danica, age ten, never liked participating in sports or group exercises because she said she was "no good at them." She would scoff at the very mention of a baseball, soccer, or basketball match, and she had a negative attitude. To make matters worse, in gym class, she was usually the last person to be chosen for any team.

Her parents brought her to me to suggest a form of exercise. I recommended bike riding, which appeared to interest her. Her parents bought her a brand new bike to ride every weekend. In follow-up sessions, her parents said Danica now loved riding the bike. They said she was still not interested in team sports, but they were happy that she was now pursuing some form of physical activity outside the home.

There's so much emphasis on team sports in our culture that it might be easy to forget that there are alternative ways to become physically fit. Some children and adults are never ready for team sports. Some personalities are a better fit with individual sports.

Remember, sports can be individual (golf, tennis, running) or team (soccer, basketball, baseball, hockey). Both types offer health benefits, and if your child doesn't enjoy traditional team sports, perhaps an individual sport will be more to his liking.

COMPETITION

The level of competitiveness can vary depending on whether or not a sport is team-oriented or geared toward an individual. Many team sports are more competitive. Even amongst teams there may be a difference in the level of competitiveness—some groups or leagues are simply more competitive than others. In basketball, soccer, and baseball you'll find town, school, and travel teams. The town and school teams in your community will usually be less competitive and require less of a time commitment. In some sports, "pickup games" are an alternative to forming an actual team, and these are often available in middle schools, high schools, local YMCAs, Boys and Girls Clubs, or places of worship. The games are held on regular occasions and anyone can drop in and play. In addition, many communities offer free clinics sponsored by town, city, or sports organizations, during the summer or year-round.

> Eleven-year-old Ray came to see me with his mother. She was very concerned about her son's lack of physical activity and wanted some guidance to help him become more active. Ray told me that he had never liked team sports and had quit Little League and soccer at age eight. He had tried a season of basketball, but he didn't want to return to that either. His mother mentioned that several of Ray's friends were quite active in various sports, and that his older brother was a star soccer player. Ray told me he was not good at any sports and that he felt inadequate.

Ray represents a great number of youngsters who do not like to participate in team sports. They deem themselves slow, uncoordinated, or wholly non-athletic. While their parents worry about their children's lack of interest in team sports and their reluctance to participate in them, the children are worrying about gym in school. Our society places a premium on start athletes. If a child is unathletic, she often feels inadequate. The teasing for such children can begin as early as kindergarten.

CHARACTERISTICS OF THE UNNATURAL ATHLETE

- They fear public failure or embarrassment.
- They are naturally shy.
- They worry about letting their parents down.
- They are cautious by nature, and are often afraid of injury or new situations.
- They are self-conscious about their physical skills or lack of them.
- They are just not interested in sports and group activities.
- They don't want to participate in sports for physical and emotional reasons.
- They are targets for teasing.

INDIVIDUAL SPORTS

Kids not interested in team or individual sports, can, however, still maintain a high level of fitness by engaging in activities that do not require competition—or even contact. There are many athletic activities that are often overlooked because they are not televised or followed closely by the media. Some of these activities are:

- Dance: ballet, Irish step dancing, line dancing, jazz, tap, modern, hip hop
- Aerobics: running, walking, step aerobics
- Resistance training
- Martial arts: karate, tai chi, judo, tai kwon do
- Swimming
- Cycling

- Hiking
- Riding scooters
- Skateboarding
- Skiing
- Snowboarding
- Horseback riding
- Waterskiing
- Windsurfing

Enjoyment garnered from any of these activities will likely turn kids on to increasing their physical activity and fitness, and can possibly lead towards other athletic interests. There are often classes held at schools, health clubs, or other organizations. These include various aerobics classes, kickboxing, or dance classes. Such classes may be perfectly suited for the "unnatural athlete," as there is a social aspect and there is no competition involved.

Feel free to expose your child to a variety of activities. Every day can be different and fun. Remember: Make it fun!

HOW TO TURN A SEDENTARY CHILD INTO AN ACTIVE, INVOLVED PERSON

The best way to get your child active is to set a good example. Get out and get fit yourself! Schedule family physical activity together at least one time per week. Take it slow and gradually increase your frequency to three to four times per week, thirty minutes at a time.

Also keep in mind that children may not seek out activities on their own. It is up to parents to help their children discover new and different activities that will fit their schedule and lifestyle. Once this has begun, your child may become attached to the time together and the activity itself.

And please keep your expectations realistic. Most kids never become powerful athletes, but they can become and remain fit, healthy, and happy.

ENCOURAGE YOUR CHILD TO PARTICIPATE IN SPORTS

- *Teach your child that he doesn't need to be "the best."* Being part of the team, wearing a uniform, going for pizza with teammates, and enjoying a great game have nothing to do with how many times he struck out or scored a goal, touchdown, or a homerun.
- *Praise effort, not outcome.* Get into the habit of mentioning the effort you saw and the progress you noted in your child's skill level.
- *Cheer for the home team.* This means your child. Remind your child of whatever she is doing well, including the talents she exhibits outside of sports.
- *Talk with the coach if necessary.* In this manner, your child's coach will be sensitive and responsive to your child's issues.
- *Recognize when it is time to try another activity.* When your child is no longer having fun, it is probably time to explore another option. It is just a matter of finding the right sport or physical activity for your child.
- *Limit your child's unnecessary sedentary activity (TV, computer).* For my children the rule is: if it's nice outside, they are outside.
- *Join a gym, or hire a personal trainer for your child.*

Q&A WITH DR. SMALL

My sixteen-year-old daughter has started taking yoga classes with her friends. She stretches in all kinds of positions and directions and because she is not naturally agile, I worry that this could be dangerous. Should she consider something else, for her own safety?

A For most people, yoga is an excellent workout for the body. Yoga encourages mental strength as well as physical flexibility. Under proper tutelage, yoga is not dangerous for those of any body build. If your daughter is performing the exercises improperly, however, she may be at risk of pulling or tearing muscles. The best way to measure the safety and effectiveness of a yoga class is by gauging the comfort level of the participant. If your daughter seems comfortable with the yoga postures, then she has found a good activity. Remember, "no pain, no gain" is *not* the yoga philosophy. The positions and the stretches should not hurt—if they do, she should find another instructor. Be mindful, too, that yoga only promotes muscle strength and flexibility; it does not enhance heart and lung fitness.

Q *My son is uncoordinated and cautious, and has not discovered an athletic activity that is suitable for him, even though he longs to be active and part of a team. I don't want him to be categorized as a "nerd" or left sitting on a bench. Can you suggest a meaningful activity for such a child?*

A There are activities that your son can do in a group without being involved in a competitive team sport. Resistance training, running, swimming, or martial arts are all done in a group or public setting, yet your son would still be training for and against himself rather than for a team.

Another way your child can be part of a team is to become a team manager or a sports writer for the school newspaper. Although this cannot replace the need for your son to be physically active, he can still be part of the "team spirit."

Q *I am not a good fitness role model for my children. I am overweight and have never been interested in sports, even as a young child. My children, now ages two to nine, have not shown any interest either, and I think I am partially to blame. Is there some way that I can get them interested and involved?*

A You are correct in saying sedentary parents may have a hard time motivating their children to stay fit. I know it may be hard for you to change lifelong habits, but you can all work together to become more fit and develop your own family spirit as opposed to a team spirit. Start with a family walk or hike through your local park. Not only would your family become more fit together, but you would also gain some important family time. Any activity that your family decides on would be great! Take it slow and gradually increase your frequency to three to four times per week, thirty minutes at a time. By creating a supportive environment and acting as a role model to whatever extent you can manage, you can help your children develop lifetime good health habits.

Q *I enjoy specific sports that I would like to share with my child, but he's not terribly interested in sports. I don't want to put pressure on my non-athletic child, but I want him to be healthy. What do you think I should do?*

A There is no reason why you shouldn't share your own personal interests or experiences in sports with your child, but keep in mind that just because you enjoyed a sport or once excelled in it does not mean your child will be interested in it, too. But you can certainly try.

Q *I live in the city and have young children. I have errands to run and chores on the weekend. I cannot just send the kids to play in the backyard. What should I do?*

A Perhaps your young children can walk with you while you do your errands. The pace will be slower, yet your children will be getting both exercise and special time with their parent.

Q *I have a five-year-old son. For physical reasons, I am unable to participate in the physical activities appropriate for my child. What do you suggest I do?*

A It is unfortunate that you are not able to do these physical activities with your child. But you can still support your child's interest in exercise by enrolling him in various sports or exercise programs. You may want to try to get a relative or an adult friend who lives nearby to work on skills with your son—throwing, kicking, or hitting a ball. Your interest and involvement will be very important to him, whether you're on the field or on the sidelines cheering him on.

CHAPTER NINE

THE CHILD WITH A CHRONIC DISEASE

Five-year-old Athena skipped into my office and jumped onto my examination table. She waited patiently as her mother told me how Athena tired easily and didn't want to participate in any sports.

"I want to do sports, Mom," she interjected, "but I just get out of breath so fast." To look at Athena, anyone would find it hard to believe that an active, inquisitive child could get so quickly winded. I asked her to tell me more, and she said, "All the kids run around as long as they want, and all I do is get tired out."

Her mother went on to explain that Athena was always out of breath after a game of tag or a hike up a hill, and although she had an intermittent cough, the cough became more intense and she even seemed to gasp for air after ordinary childhood activity.

I explained to Athena and her mother that she displayed the classic symptoms of exercise-induced asthma. After I performed an exercise-induced asthma test for confirmation, I discovered that her lung volume had dropped by 50 percent! (In a non-asthmatic child, there would be no drop in lung volume.) That was when we all knew why Athena didn't want to run!

ASTHMA: IT TAKES YOUR BREATH AWAY

From a young age, children with asthma often avoid physical activity because they are uncomfortable and cannot keep up with their friends. It is up to you, the parent, along with your child's physician, to recognize the symptoms of asthma or exercise-induced asthma, learn how to manage the disease with exercise, and encourage your kids to participate in physical activity.

Asthma is a condition in which the airways in the lungs constrict in response to various circumstances (viruses, cold air, physical or emotional stress). Children often have their first breathing problem anywhere from age one to age four. Airways get constricted, inflamed, and filled with mucus. Most asthma cases can be managed with medication as soon as the first symptoms appear. Other more chronic or severe cases may require daily ingestion of one or two medications. Symptoms of asthma may worsen or improve during puberty.

As many as 6 to 7 percent of American children have asthma (also known as reactive airway disease), and a whopping 80 to 90 percent of this population suffers from breathing problems with exercise. To add to this significant statistic, over 10 percent of non-asthmatics have exercise-induced asthma, or bronchoconstriction, that develops with exercise. This means that 15 percent of our youthful population has varying degrees of breathing problems that interfere with exercise.

Some professionals and many laymen think that asthmatics should simply not exert themselves. They obviously did not watch Jackie Joyner Kersee win gold medals in the heptathalon at the 1988 and 1992 Olympics! Kersee's asthma is managed with proper medication and well-defined training. Although most kids will not go on to win a gold medal like Kersee, your asthmatic child can still achieve satisfying physical performance.

Taking Notice: Recognizing the Symptoms

Children with exercise-induced asthma may have a variety of signs and symptoms. These include coughing, shortness of breath, or chest pain with exercise. Other signs include fatigue, wheezing, lips that turn white, or a tightness in the throat. Your child may not like to run or may prefer to play a position in a sport that is more sedentary, such as a goalie in soccer or hockey.

Taking Control: What You Can Do

Asthmatic children can participate in all sports, as long as they learn to manage their condition well. Although athletes can appear to have totally normal breathing patterns before activity, they could be left with significant shortness of breath during and after exercise. This shortness of breath can significantly alter their sports performance and exercise tolerance.

Before any athletic event or practice, athletes with asthma should do the following:

- Take two puffs on a prescribed inhaler ten to fifteen minutes before the activity to prevent an asthma attack and/or the early onset of fatigue.
- Put a scarf or muffler around the face to hold in heat and moisture.
- Avoid competition if it is very cold outside.
- Keep a daily log of peak flow measurement of air before, during, and after activity. If the airflow is low, two extra inhalation puffs from the inhaler may be needed or intense exercise may have to be avoided altogether.
- Make use of warm-up time to build in a period of breathing stability before beginning the event.
- Consider the regional air quality on the day before the athlete begins his conditioning. On beautiful spring days, there can be a host of allergy antagonists in the air, and during hot

summer days where the ozone layer is thick, outside exercise may need to be curtailed entirely. If the athlete chooses to work out in either case, the appropriate medications must be available should an attack occur. Before any of these options are considered, however, you and your child should consult with your physician about specific situations.

- There is a correlation between bronchospasm and the temperature and humidity of the exercise environment. Heat and water loss may also contribute to symptoms, and short intense bouts of exercise lasting four to ten minutes are most likely to trigger an asthma attack.

- A child who has not had enough to drink during the day (see Chapter Fourteen: Nutritional Guidance for the Active Child) may be somewhat dehydrated. This child is more likely to have breathing problems with exercise and experience shortness of breath and fatigue.

Early this year, I received a phone call from a father who lived in Des Moines. His son, age twelve, played competitive ice hockey and was diagnosed as a diabetic at age five. He had played ice hockey well the last seven years, but recently things had begun to change. Now, the father said, the boy often became tired and lightheaded during practice and games, and his average blood glucose levels had increased as well. His father also told me that he had grown three inches over the summer and his appetite had increased with all the activity and growth. The worried father called to ask why his son's blood sugar was so high, despite the obvious signs of health and growth.

I told the father that this scenario was typical when diabetic kids enter adolescence. Diabetic kids often pay less attention to a well-chosen diet, and they may not be as vigilant about taking regular blood sugar tests.

In order for his son to perform at his desired level, he must carefully monitor his blood sugar before meals, and before and after exercise. A journal might be a helpful tool for him; keeping a careful record of diet and exercise is useful for adults and children. Adolescence is a tough time for children to focus under the best of conditions, but children with diabetes need more support and encouragement to manage the condition as they go through their daily routine.

DIABETES: CHILDREN CAN CONTROL IT

Diabetes is a medical condition in which a person has problems regulating the blood sugar levels (glucose) in the body. Symptoms may include excessive hunger, excessive thirst, and frequent urination. Other symptoms may be abdominal pain, nausea, vomiting, and excessive weight gain or weight loss. Doctors have identified two types of diabetes: Type I (insulin dependent) and Type II (non-insulin dependent). Children generally have Type I diabetes, although in the past ten years the numbers of children with Type II diabetes has increased, probably because more children are overweight. Diabetes is a lifelong condition and not curable at this time, though medical progress is being made.

When used together, exercise, nutrition, and medication produce the right combination needed for healthy living with diabetes. Your child can control blood glucose with exercise. Exercise is particularly important in keeping the blood sugar levels in better control. In turn, there is a good chance that a lower blood sugar level might reduce the need for insulin, although it would definitely not eliminate this requirement altogether. Remember that lower blood sugar levels will have benefits later in life, such as a slightly decreased risk of eye and cardiovascular problems.

Normal blood sugar levels for diabetics should be between 60–200 milligrams/deciliter (mg/dl). If the numbers are too low—under 60— a snack is necessary. If the numbers are too high—over 200—your child should not perform routine exercise because her sugar level is not stable enough. Instead, more insulin may be required. A blood sugar level of about 120 is ideal.

If a diabetic's blood sugar level is in the normal level, between 60–200 mg/dl, the body and muscles work best. At this range, your child can exercise for a longer period of time without displaying symptoms. All diabetic children need to check their blood sugar levels every thirty to sixty minutes while exercising and within thirty minutes after completion of exercise. Children with lower blood sugar levels, however, need to be a bit more conscientious by checking their blood sugar levels a bit sooner than children with higher levels of blood sugar. Remember: Exercise lowers blood sugar, and with a low normal sugar level, the blood sugar levels could drop precipitously. If your diabetic child does not reduce his insulin dose before exercise, the serum glucose concentration will decrease naturally and produce a hypoglycemic reaction (low blood sugar). This condition will reduce energy, physical capabilities, and even affect other hormone secretions, causing an unsafe reaction and organ disruptions.

As parents of a diabetic child, there are certain signs of hypoglycemia during exercise you should always be aware of:

- A jittery feeling
- Lack of concentration
- Nervousness
- Heart palpitations
- Dizziness

If any of these symptoms are present, your child's blood sugar should be tested. (Blood sugar is tested by a finger stick with a small lancet.) If the blood sugar is low (less than 60 mg/dl) then a small snack should be given—juice, half a sandwich, or a piece of fruit, for example. If the blood sugar is still too low, the child should be seen by a physician.

The Goodstein family brought nine-year-old Sarah to see me. Sarah had suffered brain damage at birth, which caused her to have many coordination and agility problems. She was not able to stand on her own until age eight. Unfortunately, doctors had been unable to give the family a diagnosis or a name for her condition. But, with a great deal of pride and encouragement from her family, Sarah had learned to use a walker.

Her sedentary life, however, had led to excessive weight gain—so much in the last year that Sarah now faced more physical challenges. It was now even difficult for her to do the sorts of physical activity that most children her age were able to do.

Fortunately, Sarah's parents were interested in helping her develop as much fitness as her disabling condition would permit. "Help us to give her more of an edge," the father asked. "We fully understand that physical activity is much more challenging for her than our other children, but she needs to make the effort." I heartily agreed.

My first suggestion was to get her walking on a flat surface two to three times per week. A flat surface was surprisingly difficult to find, as her family lived in a hilly section of town. In addition, Sarah's parents both worked long hours outside the home, making the task even more complicated.

We decided the best time to get Sarah walking would be on the weekends. Her parents began taking her to an indoor mall during cold or inclement weather and outdoor tracks when the weather was good. She became a regular at one high school track, and saw the same friendly people every week.

Her parents also purchased a special bike, the cost of which was supplemented by insurance. Sarah is now meeting new goals (attending summer camp and participating in a dance program), goals she never thought were within her capability.

THE PHYSICALLY CHALLENGED CHILD

Children who are physically challenged usually have a tougher time becoming physically active than other children. No matter what the diagnosis (cerebral palsy, spina bifida, or other neuromuscular disorders) these kids tire easily and often have decreased performance after a short period of time. Grown-ups often mistakenly treat these kids delicately, which hinders their ability to attempt physical challenges. In spite of all the obstacles, sports participation is as necessary for these children as it is for everyone else. The best reason for participation is that it can provide a substantive boost to their self-esteem. As with Sarah, it is good to start with low intensity and short duration exercises so a child does not become overwhelmed at the onset. Your best choice is to begin slowly, and then gradually increase the length of activity so your child is exercising twenty to thirty minutes at least twice a week. Please remember that it could take a month, a year, or even many years, to get to this point of steady activity, depending upon the physical and mental condition of your child, as well as his level of determination.

Over the past decade, new and improved equipment—from wheelchairs and walkers to bicycles and snow skis—has been designed. There are wheelchair basketball leagues and tennis leagues for children in many communities, as well as other community activities such as the March of Dimes and the Special Olympics.

If you are the parent of a physically challenged child, make it your business to contact these different groups—they can all offer varying areas of support, as well as help your child to become more physically fit.

Q&A WITH DR. SMALL

Q *Are some sports better for an asthmatic child than others?*

A Studies show that swim training can actually improve the fitness of asthmatic children. Asthmatics generally do well with swimming, since that activity is done in a warm and damp environment. Conversely, they tend to be less successful with sports set in cold environments, such as hockey and skiing—the cold, combined with the exercise, is more likely to cause a bronchoconstriction (closing of the airways). Training sessions of cycling and running can also assist in improving the asthmatic child's cardiorespiratory fitness. With proper management, an asthmatic child can participate in any activity.

Q *What are common symptoms of exercise-induced asthma?*

A Dry cough, shortness of breath, fatigue, and being significantly out of breath after a brief period of exercise are frequent symptoms of exercise-induced asthma. Unfortunately, a child may be labeled as lazy or out of shape by a coach simply because she can't keep up with the activities. Hopefully, coaches will be trained to better recognize the signs of exercise-induced asthma and inform the parents whenever there is a possibility of it.

Q *The doctor gave my child an inhaler to treat his asthma, with the instructions to take two puffs prior to exercise. What if he is still short of breath during exercise?*

A You may then try two more puffs, and that should do the trick. It is unusual for this amount of medication not to work, and if it doesn't you must then consult with your doctor about additional medication.

Q *Will my child outgrow exercise-induced asthma?*

A Children may have less severe symptoms of asthma as they grow older. They will, however, always have a propensity for their airways to constrict with varying intensities of exercise. Parents should be ever watchful while their child is young, and as they grow, children must remain vigilant as well.

Q How do you perform a test for exercise-induced asthma?

A First your doctor will measure your child's breathing volume while the child is at rest. Then your child will ride on a stationary bicycle or treadmill for eight minutes, beginning at a slow speed and increasing to a moderate speed and finally escalating to a significant intensity (80 percent of predicted heart rate for age). After exercise, the child's lung volume is measured at five, ten, and fifteen minutes after exercise. If there is a drop in lung volume of more than 10 percent, your child will be diagnosed with exercise-induced asthma.

Q What are the best sports for diabetic children?

A Diabetic children can choose any sport of interest. If your child is just getting started or has recently been diagnosed with diabetes, it is best to pick a sport that is "continuous" in nature, such as walking, biking, cycling, or swimming. With these "continuous" sports, there is an easily calculated and well monitored expenditure of energy, and you can tell within close range how much glucose will be used.

Another means to promote physical activity in your child might be to send him to a specialty camp specifically geared for kids with diabetes. These camps are staffed by medical professionals who have special training in diabetes and the difficulties that surround it. It might be constructive for your child to know that other kids have the same needs, and this could be helpful in the quest to become more physically active throughout a lifetime.

Keep in mind that blood sugar needs to be measured before and after exercise to monitor a diabetic athlete's health. As we saw in the

2000 Olympics, diabetic athlete Gary Hall, Jr., won an Olympic gold medal in swimming. His preparedness clearly showed that this disease can be adequately managed, even for people who want to push the limits of activity.

Q *Will my son with diabetes always have to monitor his blood glucose before, during, and after exercise? He's thirteen years old and is complaining that it's becoming a burden to him.*

A Unfortunately, there is no way of avoiding blood glucose monitoring at the time of exercise. Since your son is thirteen, it is particularly important that you stress the necessity of monitoring. It is during the adolescent years that diabetes becomes particularly hard to manage because of the almost requisite rebellion of a teen. It is the unusual adolescent who immediately accepts total responsibility for his disease and his responses.

I suggest that parents of every diabetic child remind their youngsters that the longer they stay active and vigilant about a healthy lifestyle, the better their chances will be when future discoveries in the treatment and cure of diabetes are widely available. With continual research, there is good reason to expect a cure at some point in the future.

Q *We would like to get our child, who has spina bifida, to be more active, but we don't know where to turn. He currently walks with crutches. Do you have any suggestions?*

A There are many choices for possible activity, depending on what resources are available in your community and what your child's goals are.

If your child has muscle weakness and poor endurance, a physical therapist can work on these skills. Physical and occupational therapy may help your child to improve his level of functioning, including increasing his range of motion and strengthening the body with exercises. In some states, such as New York, public schools are mandated by law to provide services of this nature for your child. A call to your local Board of Education would clarify services to which you would be entitled.

If you are looking for more recreational activity for your child, check to see if you are lucky enough to have a special children's rehabilitation hospital in your community. These hospitals often have recreational programs for children with all types of disabilities. They also have special therapists and trainers that work with kids and sometimes prepare them for the Special Olympics. You also may want to contact the rehab department at your local hospital, the March of Dimes, Easter Seals, or Cerebral Palsy Foundation in your community.

Q *Are there any specific precautions during exercise or sports that I should take to protect my child who has a physical disability?*

A If your child complains of pain or soreness in a muscle or a joint, then that activity should be stopped or the intensity should be lessened. The next time your child does that activity, the intensity should start out at a much lower level. Keep in mind that children with neuromuscular problems are more prone to suffering heat cramps or heat stroke, and intensity of a program must be based on weather and varying temperature. Talk with your doctor to develop the exercise program that's right for your child.

PART III

COMMON QUESTIONS AND ANSWERS:

Preventive Medicine, Injury Rehabilitation, Nutrition, and Sports Psychology

CHAPTER TEN

WEIGHT TRAINING AND THE YOUNG ATHLETE

At a recent meeting of the American Academy of Pediatrics, a speaker who recommended resistance training, sometimes called weight training, for young athletes was rudely denounced by older members of the audience. "Totally inappropriate, downright harmful, and altogether foolish," were the words they shouted at the embarrassed speaker.

I sat there watching the group divide itself, mostly by age, in its approach to this subject, and decided to reserve my comments for this book.

Mention weight training in respect to the child athlete and you will hear any number of people—from all age groups, especially those with professional credentials—say that resistance training will stunt a child's growth.

Well-documented scientific information indicates that strength training won't inhibit a child's growth under normal circumstances. (See Resources for Parents on page 230 for further information on weight training and a child's growth.) Strength training can, however, cause injury if heavy weights are used or improper exercise techniques are employed.

When carefully supervised and correctly performed, strength training can be a perfectly safe activity for boys and girls as young as the age of eight. One study performed at the University of Massachusetts by Wayne Wescott and colleagues showed strength gains and relatively few injuries after ten weeks of weight training. In fact, strength training may actually lower a child's risk of sustaining a sports related injury, since strong muscle tissue protects the musculoskeletal system.

THE REQUIREMENTS FOR WEIGHT TRAINING

The child must show an interest in the activity.

Maturity is a key factor in carrying out a weight-training program. How do we define maturity—by age or by capability? Some eight-year-olds can profit from a weight-training program, and some twelve-year-olds cannot. The definition of maturity in this context means that the child is disciplined enough to carry out the prescribed exercises and knows enough about the process to never sacrifice technique for lifting extra weight or performing more repetitions.

Children who begin weight training must have a basic understanding of the strengths and limitations of their bodies. They must also be knowledgeable enough about the activity to know that a prepubescent boy will not significantly increase his muscle bulk until he reaches puberty. Even after puberty, many girls will not become bulky because they lack the same level of testosterone as boys. Boys and girls can, however, increase muscle strength and improve their appearance.

A young athlete must also be advised that if pain occurs while doing an exercise, all activity must stop. If the pain persists when the activity begins again, the child and the parents must consult with a physician.

The activity must be done under the supervision of a qualified adult.

Who fits the standard of "the qualified adult"? This is often a certified athletic trainer, physical therapist, or a coach—someone who has received appropriate accreditation in sports education and fitness training, and has taken the necessary course work and passed the exam given by these associations.

In addition, this person must be specifically accredited to train children, after receiving credentials from the National Strength and Conditioning Association, the American Physical Therapy Association, or the National Athletic Trainers' Association. All of these associations have certifying courses and mandated continuing education classes regarding strength training, among other important areas. It is the parents' responsibility to verify the credentials of their child's coach, as well as to ensure that the coach will provide their child with the best and safest training possible.

I recommend that you and your child observe a training session because there are many personal trainers who have little, if any, experience with children. After you and your child have observed the coach conducting a training session with another child and you both are satisfied, your child can then proceed under the direct supervision of this qualified adult. A child under incorrect supervision may suffer from growth plate injuries (injuries involving parts of the bones that are actively growing, such as the knee, ankle, lower back, and shoulder) or from headaches and muscle soreness. If your child develops a severe pain during or after a weight-training session— a limp or the inability to move a limb—she should always have the problem checked by a doctor. If the parent feels the child is being incorrectly advised or supervised, then finding a new trainer should be the first course of action. The doctor should also be advised of a pain that does not go away within a week after the weight-training session.

The practice of strength training among children must be done in adherence to a safe concept of low-weight resistance and a high number of repetitions.

Weight training refers to placing the whole body (push-ups, sit-ups) or part of the body (biceps, triceps) through resistance. In this case, it refers to placing the body muscles through minimum resistance. When dealing with children's bodies, the safest form of weight training involves low-weights combined with a high number of repetitions. Children can accomplish this by using free weights (dumbbells, barbells), weight machines (available at health clubs), and resistance bands/tubing. Some people lose sight of the fact that simple push-ups and sit-ups are a form of resistance training.

The best place to research weight training or any sports related activity is a local sports center or fitness club where certified instructors (physical therapists and athletic trainers with knowledge of the growth and development of children) are available to advise you and your child. If the child chooses to begin resistance training, a qualified instructor will set up a program, beginning with only one session per week so that the activity and the results build at a comfortable rate. Ask the instructor to choose a weight with which the child can easily perform repetitions with good technique. A good rule of thumb is to do three sets of ten repetitions of the exercise (bicep curls, triceps extension) per session. The weight used should be heavy enough to stress the muscle, but not so heavy as to place the young athlete at risk for injury. (See Chapter Thirteen: Flexibility, Strength, and Conditioning for exercises.)

Children are exposed to fitness information from magazines, television, and in doctors' offices. Although the information that children learn from these magazines and television shows may be well intentioned, it can lack scientific basis and could do a child more harm than good. For example, many workout demonstrations on television or print advertisements may appear to be safe for adults who have been working out for months or even years, but these same exercises and workout plans are not safe for children. The demonstrator often recommends a certain weight preference per machine, and this is not likely to be safe for the child. Certified instructors can help you determine what's right for your child.

Any athletic accomplishment builds confidence. For non-athletic, overweight, and disabled children, weight training can be a way to increase self-esteem and confidence.

THE BENEFITS OF WEIGHT TRAINING

There are numerous benefits to weight training for the child who is ready to begin this course of athleticism.

Improved Strength

Years ago, it was believed that a young person's strength could only be improved once the effects of testosterone and other hormones affected the muscle mass—i.e., once the child had entered puberty. But it has now been proven that even prepubescent children—male or female— can improve their strength by weight training, especially by using different muscles from ones used in their primary sport. Strength training can also enhance neurological control and response. What is equally important is that girls who practice weight training gain the same strength advantages from the training as boys do.

A recent Penn State study showed that six months of a generalized weight-training program, which focused on the upper as well as lower body, improved the velocity of forehand and backhand stroke as well as the tennis serves of female college tennis players by up to 20 percent.

Although athletic young women may recognize the obvious gain in strength brought by resistance training, many are still reluctant to try the activity for fear that they will develop "big thighs and arms." Fortunately, this is just a myth. If young females use resistance tubing/bands or low weights and high repetitions, they will just improve their muscle tone and the look of their bodies, without "bulking up."

Injury Prevention and Weight Training

What must be stressed at this point is that all children who are about to enter into a weight-training program or any other regular sports activity must be checked for physiological characteristics that could put them at risk for injuries. There are many children and adolescents who suffer from muscle imbalance or have one set of muscles that are not strong enough to meet the demands of their chosen activity. Properly supervised weight training is ideal for correcting muscle imbalance.

In runners, for instance, the inner aspect of the thigh muscle (the quadriceps) may not be as developed as it should be. If the young athlete can work to strengthen this muscle, he will be better able to prevent knee injury. In overhand sports, such as tennis, baseball, and swimming, the muscles that pull the shoulder forward are very strong in direct comparison to the muscles that draw the shoulder back. Strengthening exercises, done with free weights that work on the back of the shoulder and upper back, will do a lot to prevent shoulder injury. In ballet, the muscles (plantar flexors) that pull the foot down are very strong, in comparison to the muscles that draw the foot up (dorsiflexors). Exercises are necessary to strengthen the dorsiflexors.

Improved Self-Esteem

One of the most important benefits of weight training is not only the physical but also the psychological advantages of a fit and strengthened body. This issue has far reaching consequences for many children. For the athlete with exceptional capabilities, it's a given that fitness affords an edge in competition.

For the non-athlete, the overweight, undersized, or disabled child, the additional body strength and the confidence may be just the right impetus for that child to try and succeed at a team sport.

BIGGER IS NOT BETTER

Even modest strength gains may take as long as six weeks to achieve. But strength itself is not necessarily quantified by an increase in muscle size. Strength can be based solely on the increased amount of weight one can lift or by the number of repetitions one is able to do.

As we have stressed, weight training can be an excellent part of a youngster's healthy exercise program. It is a safe and beneficial activity if proper techniques and precautions are taken. Awareness of what the young athlete is doing in terms of training and whom she is working with is a large part of the parent's responsibility.

Unfortunately, many adolescent boys are only interested in getting "bigger" muscles, not necessarily getting healthier or stronger. They must be advised to increase their muscle mass with proper training routines and optimum nutrition, not with muscle enhancing drugs. (See Chapter Fifteen: Nutritional Supplements and Steroids.) Parents, teachers, and coaches must remain closely involved with the young athlete's sports program and be aware of the child's goals and specific training regimen.

The child who uses sports to his advantage and has the complete cooperation and the ear of all the adults involved avoids most of the risks and problems that could occur without the right supervision.

Elise was a competitive figure skater. Although graceful and adept and well on her way to regional championships, Elise had grown in two years from 5' 1" at age twelve to 5' 5½" by age fourteen. Her height and her ever-so-slightly-fuller figure hindered the agile and flowing movement she needed to accomplish the skills of the sport. Elise fell continuously as she tried to improve her jumps and spins. Her body was no longer her ally since her weight and height had shifted her body balance.

Disheartened by her lack of accomplishment on the ice, she and her mother came to me to discuss alternatives. After a tearful recounting of her travails, she said her "life in sports was over." I agreed that perhaps her competitive skating days were over, but her opportunities to thrive in other sports were just beginning.

During our visit, we discussed other sports that she enjoyed, which included running. Although she had fun with this activity, she told me that she had never attempted any competitive track or cross-country running. She listened carefully as I told her about some additional training elements that would literally get her "up to speed" in a short time.

We immediately added resistance training to Elise's running regimen, and she was soon lifting light weights in a smooth and slow manner, while increasing repetition. She also worked out with weights on her upper and lower body on alternative days. Within a fairly short period of time, Elise had increased her resistance exercise by three-fold and her endurance runs by two-fold—enough strength and speed to place her in regional track competitions.

Now at age fifteen and a half, Elise is happily competing on a state level in cross-country running and is grateful that her ice skating days began the preparation for the skills and motivation needed in her current sport.

WEIGHT TRAINING: A WARNING

There are a number of strength enhancement exercises that are clearly NOT recommended for young athletes. These exercises are meant for those grown men and women who compete in this skill alone. They are:

- The clean and jerk (an Olympic over-the-head lift)
- Maximum lifts
- Butterflies

The necessary skills for the child athlete to keep in mind and build into any weight training session are:

- To work on opposing muscle groups, one after the other
- To increase muscle endurance
- To begin any strength enhancing workout with aerobic warm-up

- To never sacrifice form or technique

Weight training is ideal for the child who is active in different sports all year round and wants to prevent injury. It is also good for children who play competitive sports all year round. A child who participates in many sports or the child who competes in one sport may improve his conditioning by incorporating weight training and aerobic exercise. By working on diverse athletics in this manner, the child gains from the flexibility, strength, experience, and enjoyment—not the overuse of the body.

Sample Strength-Training Workout

A) Engage in five to ten minutes of aerobic warm-up (jogging, a brisk walk, jumping jacks, jumping rope—any activity that moderately raises the heart rate).

B) Engage in several minutes of stretching the upper and lower body. Stretches should be held for fifteen to twenty seconds without bobbing. (See Chapter Thirteen: Flexibility, Strength, and Conditioning.)

C) Do three sets of ten bicep curls starting with a comfortable weight.* (See Figure 7, page 158.)

D) Do three sets of ten tricep extensions starting with a comfortable weight.* (See Figure 8, page 158.)

E) Do three sets of ten knee extension/knee flexions.* (See Figures 13 & 14, page 161.)

F) Allow for several minutes of stretching to complete the routine.

*All of these exercises can be completed with any of the following three pieces of equipment:

1) Resistance bands
2) Free weights
3) Weight machines

Every two to three weeks, your child can increase the number of repetitions by a set of ten, or increase the weight by 10 percent.

Q&A WITH DR. SMALL

Q My *ten-year-old son wants to start weight training because his friends are playing around with weights they have at home. I don't think the children are properly supervised, and I don't want my child to get hurt. What should I do?*

A By encouraging your son to begin weight training—but only with an accredited instructor—you can minimize the possibility of his getting hurt. You can find the appropriate teachers by asking about the people who are training young athletes in nearby sports centers. Once your son has learned the essentials and the proper way to train, he will be at less risk. Should he want to practice resistance training with his friends, he may convince them to learn the proper way as well.

Q *Are there children who should not consider weight and resistance training?*

A Most weight as well as resistance training exercises are excellent for most people. There are those, however, who should limit aggressive training of all sorts because of specific health problems, such as chronic hypertension and joint instability.

Q *Is weight training dangerous for girls?*

A Any sport or fitness activity can be made dangerous for those who don't take proper precautions. Weight training is considered safe for girls as well as boys if they practice the proper form and technique taught to them by experts. And, just like any other athletic activity, the girl must want to do the work and enjoy it as much as she likes any elective activity.

Q *Are sit-ups considered resistance training? Are they good in conjunction with weight training?*

A Sit-ups are good for both boys and girls, and when done properly they work with weights to provide upper body strength. Proper sit-ups can be done by putting your hands behind your head (see Figure 1 below) or by crossing your arms over your chest and coming forward halfway from the ground. But be careful! As in weight training, too many repetitions may cause back pain, not prevent it. Children who do as many as two hundred sit-ups a day can develop an imbalance of their abdominal muscles in relation to their lower backs. Therefore, lower-back strengthening exercises should also be introduced at this time. Keep in mind: Moderation and balance are key.

Q *Are there any weight machines designed especially for kids?*

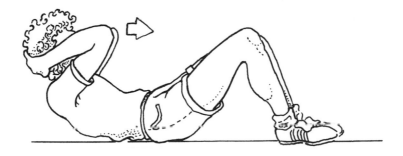

Figure 1: A proper sit-up

A Yes, a number of sports training equipment companies design weight machines and exercise bikes specifically for children. These machines take into account a child's shorter height and lighter weight. Be certain that your child does not use machines that are designed specifically for adults because improper placement of the child's limbs on the machine may cause injury to muscles, tissues, and bones.

Q *What is the difference between free weights and weight machines?*

A Free weights come in the form of dumbbells and barbells, as well as ankle and wrist weights. They wrap around the arms and legs with Velcro or are held in the hand while exercising. Machine weights function by a lever and pulley system. Both the free weights and the weight machines offer several benefits, including increased muscle strength. Weight machines and free weights are both relatively risk-free for children—that is, if the machines and individual weights are used properly, and the child is under direct supervision and never left unattended.

Q *How many times per week and how many minutes per session should my child perform resistance training?*

A Children should definitely not lift weights more that two to three times per week, and sessions should last on average twenty minutes per program, but not more than sixty minutes. A period as long as sixty minutes is only appropriate after they have been training for several months.

Q *My child says that the fitness and weight training that her coach has recommended are boring. What can we do to make it fun?*

A There are a number of things that you could try. You could have the coach do group fitness activities as part of their warm-up or practice session. When these activities are done in a group setting, they are definitely more enjoyable. Ask the coach to have a child lead the exercises, and rotate the group for leadership opportunity. If the coach is unable to do these activities, you may want to try this at home with your child and the rest of the family.

CHAPTER ELEVEN

COMMON SPORTS INJURIES:
Prevention and Management

*Thirteen-year-old Marianne came to see me three days after suf-
fering a knee injury. She had been in a travel soccer tournament
in New England over the weekend. Towards the end of the third
game on day one, she fell. The athletic trainer examined her and
told her to ice her painful knee. The next day she felt a bit better
and told the coach she wanted to play. After several minutes in
the game, Marianne caught her foot in a divet in the field trying
to change direction. She felt a pop and there was immediate
swelling; her knee and lower leg had shifted forward.*

*When I examined her, her left knee was very swollen, and
she was unable to flex or extend it. The lower leg (tibia) came
too far forward relative to her upper leg (femur) when I applied
force. She had obviously suffered a complete tear in the anterior
cruciate ligament (ACL), the major ligament that stabilizes the
knee. Without the ACL, she would not be able to run, jump,
and participate in sports.*

ACUTE INJURY

Marianne's story represents an unfortunate occurrence. However, her
serious ACL tear could possibly have been prevented if the initial

injury had been treated properly. When she tripped in the divet in the field, her already weakened knee could not hold up.

Acute injuries occur suddenly and are usually associated with some form of trauma. In younger children, acute injuries typically include minor trauma, such as bruises, moderate contusions, sprains, and strains. Teenage athletes, by virtue of the intensity of their sports, are likely to suffer more severe injuries, including broken bones and torn ligaments.

The Most Common Acute Injuries

- *Bruises/Contusions*. An injury that occurs after a fall or a bump. The result is swelling and inflammation of soft tissue, muscle, or bone.
- *Abrasions*. An injury that occurs after a scrape. The result is an injury to skin or cut.

In most cases, a parent or coach can administer simple first aid after a bruise or contusion. A visit to a physician is often not necessary.

- *Lacerations*. A tearing or breaking of the skin.
- *Sprains (ligament fibers)*. A sprain occurs when the ligaments, which hold bones together, are overstretched and partially torn. Ankle sprains are the most common type of sprain. Ninety-five percent of acute sprains are at the outside of the ankle. The treatment is to restore range of motion and strength by performing specific skills. The rehab can be accomplished by doing the exercises in an office setting with an athletic trainer or a physical therapist. Protective bracing (Ace bandage, taping, lace-up brace, or other ankle brace) is helpful.
- *Muscle strain (muscle fibers)*. An irritation, inflammation, and partial tearing of the tissues within the muscle.
- *Ligament tears*. A tear of a ligament, one of the structures that hold bones together. When an athlete tears a ligament, he

usually experiences a popping or a snapping sensation and immediate swelling. The anterior cruciate ligament (ACL), the major knee stabilizer, is commonly torn in basketball and soccer.

- *Dislocations (shoulder, knee, or finger)*. The shoulder, knee, or finger moves out of joint. This is one of the most painful experiences an athlete can have.
- *Broken bones*. This almost always requires emergency care. You are right to suspect a possible broken bone if you or your child heard or felt a bone snap. Other symptoms induce difficulty moving the injured part, if the injured part moves in an unnatural way, or if it is very painful to the touch.
- *Avulsion or chip fractures*. A piece of bone breaks off at the site of a muscle/tendon attachment (at the hip, or below the knee). This happens when a muscle tendon unit is stronger than bone; there may be a forceful contraction of a muscle group such as the hip when someone goes to kick the ball.
- *Growth plate injuries and fractures*. The growth plate is the site where bone is growing, and this point is weakest during growth spurts. A regular sprained ankle becomes a growth plate injury in a child undergoing a growth spurt. If growth plate fractures are not treated appropriately, there are can be a discrepancy between the lengths of the child's limbs—the injured leg may stop growing or not grow properly.

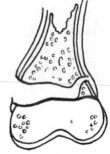

Figure 2: Growth plate fracture

For the majority of these injuries, especially when a broken bone or a torn ligament is suspected, a visit to a doctor or an emergency room is in order. Do not "force" your child to move the suspected broken leg or arm. Do not tell your child to walk if she is unable to put pressure on the injured leg.

Treatment of Acute Injuries

When an injury occurs, watch out for immediate swelling. If this happens, or if the player is incapable of performing the required sport task, then the player should stop immediately. This is where the **R.I.C.E.** principle is used: Rest, Ice, Compression, and Elevation.

- Rest. "Rest" is a relative term. It doesn't mean your child needs to sit in bed, but he must rest the injury and not make it worse. The athlete should be encouraged to use other muscles and body parts that are not injured. This is the time to try an alternative sports activity. For example, perhaps your young athlete can try swimming or biking if he is recovering from an ankle injury.
- Ice. Ice is applied to the injured area up to ten times a day for ten to fifteen minutes at a time. This will reduce the swelling. Swelling may occur at the end of the day for up to several months after a severe acute injury. It's a good idea to ice after activity or at the end of the day.
- Compression. This concept refers to placing pressure (Ace bandage, supportive taping, or other brace) around the involved joint to give it support and prevent further injury. Compression should be applied during the day and especially while trying to bear weight on the injury.
- Elevation. After an injury it is advisable to elevate the injured body part, to raise it above the heart. This will prevent pooling of fluids and more swelling. Elevation can be done four to five times per day at the same time while the injured child is icing the injured body part.

Fourteen-year-old Frank, a cross-country runner, came to me last September for an evaluation of his shin pain. His visit coincided with the beginning of school and his third season of cross-country training. He experienced pain in his shins after only one week of running. During the months of summer vacation, Frank had not run at all and had grown four inches. The previous two years he had run for one month prior to the season and had not suffered any injuries.

With a physical exam, I determined that he had diffuse pain all along his shins. His history and physical exam were compatible with a diagnosis of shin splints. It also turned out that his running shoes were six months old and worn out. His treatment was simple—cutting back his running mileage by half, strengthening his feet and ankles, and wearing a new pair of shoes.

CHRONIC/OVERUSE INJURY

Frank's story represents a typical setup for an overuse injury—inadequate training, a growth spurt, and poor equipment.

Chronic injuries, also called overuse injuries, occur gradually over time. Overuse injuries occur from repetitive actions that put too much stress on the musculoskeletal system without adequate time for recovery. Any child who plays sports can develop overuse injuries.

Most injuries that occur now are overuse injuries; these injuries in children did not exist a decade ago. Kids played sports according to the season—baseball in the spring, football in the fall, and basketball in the winter. This calendar allowed the muscles to rest. But in today's environment, kids are more scheduled and spend more time devoted to one sport; the muscles cannot rest and heal. The more time your child spends on one sport, the more likely your child is to experience an overuse injury.

In some cases, an injured child may not be able to resume his sport, temporarily, without risking further injury. In this case, another sport or activity, one which doesn't strain the affected body part, is the best way to continue your child's activity level and interests. When total recovery can be attained, adjustment in the child's technique and/or training schedule is necessary to prevent recurrence of the original injury. In other cases merely a reduction in sports activity may help treat the overuse injury.

Common Causes of Chronic/Overuse Injuries

- *Training error.* This includes doing too much, too soon, too fast, and is the most common cause of overuse injury. For example, a cross-country runner who does no running over the summer and starts running twenty miles per week in late August is at risk to suffer an overuse injury of knees, shins, or ankles.
- *Problem equipment.* As discussed earlier, worn sneakers, improperly fitted footwear, or improper sports equipment can cause injury.
- *Environmental conditions (too hot, too cold).* If it is very hot and humid outside, the youngster is likely to suffer from heat injury and dehydration. If the body is dehydrated, the muscles are also dehydrated and likely to tire more easily. Tired muscles can contribute to an injury. If it is very cold outside, the muscles lack blood flow and are not "warm." A muscle that is not "warm" is likely to be injured.
- *Nutrition.* A young athlete who goes into practice or competition without eating properly will more likely suffer from fatigue and injury.
- *Hydration.* A young athlete who goes into practice or competition without enough fluid intake before and during competition will be a prime candidate for fatigue and injury.
- *Anatomic misalignment.* Sometimes an athlete's physical condition, such as being bowlegged, knock-kneed, or having high-arched feet, can contribute to an injury. In such situation, sneakers with good arch support and a supportive heel are helpful. If a child has frequent aches and pains in the foot, then shoe inserts should be purchased with your doctor's advice.

- *Muscle imbalance*. If one muscle group is repetitively used without strengthening the others and without adequately resting the muscles, a muscle imbalance may result. For example, muscles at the front of the shoulder are much stronger than at the back of the shoulder in swimmers, baseball pitchers, and tennis players. Opposing muscles include: biceps/triceps, shoulder internal/external rotation, knee extension/flexion, and foot plantarflexion/dorsiflexion.
- *Growth spurt*. During a growth spurt, the muscles tighten up and become less flexible. The athlete becomes less coordinated and less fluid. This may cause injury.
- *Prior injury*. An athlete who has a chronic injury or one that has not been properly treated and rehabilitated is vulnerable to injury.
- *Deconditioning*. This term refers to being "out of shape"—the athlete's heart and lung fitness, as well as muscle strength, are not what they should be.

The Most Common Chronic Overuse Injuries

There are many chronic overuse injuries that limit an athlete's ability to improve. The most frequent of these are:

- *Shin splints*. This term refers to microscopic tearing of muscles where they attach to the bone on the shins. Pain, inflammation, and irritation result along the lower parts of the legs. The cause is usually due to repeated running on hard surfaces. Treatment requires a decrease of running mileage and decreasing participation in sports by 30 percent over a two to four week period.

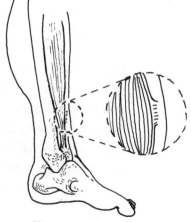

Figure 3: Shin splints

- *Osgood-Schlatter Disease.* This condition occurs during a growth spurt, usually ages twelve to fifteen for boys and ages nine to twelve for girls. It is a pain of the tibia tubercle bone, just below the kneecap. Treatment is leg lifts and hamstring stretches. (See pages 134–136 and 142 for more information about this condition.)

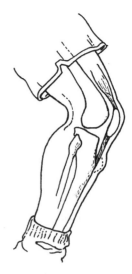

Figure 4: Osgood-Schlatter

- *Patella Femoral Pain Syndrome.* This is also called runner's knee. It is a pain in and around the kneecap. In severe cases, there is swelling; in the majority of cases, there is only pain while running or walking up and down stairs. Treatment requires a decrease in running by 30 to 50 percent, along with leg lifts for support.

- *Shoulder subluxation.* This is a condition of abnormal movement within the shoulder joint itself, which is the result of weak shoulder muscles holding the joint in place. It may be a result of strong muscles in the front and weaker muscles in the back of the shoulder. Treatment consists of shoulder and upper back strengthening.

- *Swimmer's shoulder.* An inflammation of the shoulder caused by repeated stress of the overhead motion, commonly associated with swimming. The pain starts out as intermittent discomfort and can escalate to continuous distress. Treatment requires decreasing the swimming yardage, doing more breaststroke instead of freestyle or butterfly, and increasing shoulder and upper back strengthening.

- *Little League Shoulder.* This injury is the result of repetitive microtrauma caused by the explosive dynamic forces of the athletic activity, such as the pitching motion. Treatment requires no throwing for four to six weeks, as well as shoulder strengthening.

- *Little League Elbow.* The injury is caused by repetitive throwing, causing pain and tenderness in the inner aspect of the elbow region. The ability to flex and extend the elbow may become more and more limited without treatment. If untreated, this condition may lead to bone chips and arthritis twenty years or more down the road. Treatment also requires no throwing for six to twenty-four weeks, as well as wrist and forearm strengthening.
- *Sever's Disease.* This condition causes pain in the heel, where the Achilles tendon inserts into the heel. It usually occurs in boys ages ten to twelve and girls ages eight to ten. It is the result of tight muscles in the heel and a growth spurt. Treatment requires stretching the affected area.
- *Stress fracture of lower body (shin, foot, or toes).* This is an injury to the bone resulting from playing impact sports without permitting the body enough time to recover. Treatment requires that the athlete avoid running, jumping, or other impact activities for two to six weeks. Occasionally a walking boot is needed to expedite healing.
- *Stress fracture of the lower back (spondylolysis).* This is a stress fracture or an acute fracture of the back portion of the vertebrae (pars interarticularis). The condition is associated with sports that require repetitive hyperextension or twisting of the lower back, such as gymnastics, figure skating, dance, football (particularly the position of lineman), and racquet sports. Treatment requires back bracing for three to nine months and formalized physical therapy.

Thirteen-year-old Matthew was the star catcher on his Little League team. Despite his enjoyment of the game and the strength he brought to his team, he complained regularly about pain in his knees. His parents took him to his pediatrician, who diagnosed his problem as simple "growing pains" and offered no suggestions for relief of the pain, except over-the-counter anti-inflammatory medication.

Matthew was clearly upset when he told me about his problem. After reviewing Matthew's medical history and performing a complete physical exam, it was clear that, in fact, he suffered from Osgood-Schlatter Disease—an overuse injury that leads to swelling and tenderness below the knee. The name of the condition frightened Matthew and his mother—that is, until they learned it was a fancy name for a condition that is easily treated. Simply put: the prototypical "growing pain."

In conjunction with muscle strengthening and flexibility and stretching exercises for his hamstrings and quadriceps, Matthew was also required to change positions on his team because the combination of squatting and his rapid growth contributed to his condition. The team coach assigned Matthew the position of first base, where the necessary motions would not add to Matthew's problem.

Within a month, Matthew's pain had subsided considerably and he was again ready to play one to two innings as a catcher. By summer, he was ready to catch an entire game. Matthew and his coach agreed that he needed to be careful not to re-injure his knees, and he promised to report any pain, should it reoccur.

Although growing pains could have temporarily sidetracked Matthew's Little League experience, the coach and Matthew's parents considered the teenager's bout of Osgood-Schlatter Disease to be a good learning experience, as well as a positive period of emotional growth.

YOUR CHILD'S "GROWING PAINS"

Did you ever wake up in the morning, look at your child, and swear that she grew overnight? You could be right. And with that growth spurt may have come some irritating aches and pains in the hips, legs, knees, and shins. Your grandparents probably called this discomfort "growing pains," and they were not far from the truth.

Children do grow in spurts, and during these times, bones grow more quickly than muscles and tendons, while flexibility temporarily decreases. That is often why children come home from school sports or camp activities in varying degrees of pain. There are basically two types of growing pains:

1. From ages four to ten, children may wake up at night, screaming of pain, and there is no swelling or tenderness surrounding the affected body part. These pains generally go away within weeks. If there is persistent pain, the parent should take the child to his physician.

2. From ages ten to fifteen, pain affects specific parts of the body where muscle/tendon units attach to growing bones. This occurs with Osgood-Schlatter Disease (pain where the patella tendon inserts into the tibia tubercle), Sever's Disease (pain where the Achilles tendon inserts into the heel bone), and Little League Elbow (pain at the inner aspect of the elbow). There are specific findings on exam, such as extreme pain at muscle tendon bone junction, often accompanied by swelling. For this type of growing pain, specific treatment protocols need to be instituted. Strengthening, stretching, and activity monitoring are all essential requirements for treatment. (See Chapter Thirteen: Flexibility, Strength, and Conditioning.)

Often the activities that require growing children to squat, jump, lunge, and run place stress on the underlying muscles and cause inflammation. Parents and coaches also refer to this period of growth as "an awkward phase." This is a truly accurate assessment. The young athlete's balance, coordination, and relative muscle strength are often diminished during this time. In addition, the rate of injury can increase and the young athlete's performance is often decreased.

For example, a basketball player who grew five inches during a summer break may not dribble down the court as adeptly as before. Similarly, the gymnast who grew just as fast may not be able to complete a floor routine with the same fluidity as before. It may take up to one year for flexibility, balance, and coordination to return. Patience is key for anyone who works and cares for these children.

PREVENTING INJURY

About half of children's injuries that occur during organized sports activities are preventable, and the most common sports injuries are re-injuries. Re-injury occurs when an athlete returns to a sport before the injury has sufficiently healed, and recovery isn't complete. This forces the body to compensate for the weak spot. In addition to this re-injury, the athlete is now likely to injure an adjacent body part.

Make sure your child prevents re-injury by properly warming up and stretching before exercise and cooling down after exercise. Your child should also pace himself, since sudden exertion can also cause re-injury. Explain to your child that easing back into his sport at a sensible pace is better than returning to the sidelines.

You can help your youngster prevent sports injuries, re-injuries, and chronic injury by following some simple rules:

1) Use proper equipment.
Sports equipment that is carefully fitted for your child is essential for injury prevention. If your child is involved in baseball, softball, hockey, or cycling, outfit your child with helmets with polycarbonate shields. You'd also be wise to provide her with protective eyewear for basketball and racket sports. Ask your child's coach about appropriate helmets, mouth guards, and padding.

Proper footwear is also extremely important. For a child who has a very low arch and flat feet, extra padding in the sneaker or an over-the-counter orthotic device (such as a shoe insert) is helpful. If a child's sneakers or cleats begin to wear out, they should be replaced immediately.

Athletic equipment should be safety-oriented. Newer "breakaway" bases that move when hit by a sliding player, for example, have been effective in reducing leg injuries caused by sliding into a base. It is also smart to inquire about the maintenance of all equipment to make sure it's effective.

2) Maintain safe playing surfaces.

Check that playing fields or tracks are clean flat surfaces. If there are cracks and ruts in the way, there is always a chance that a child will take a bad spill.

3) Ensure adequate adult supervision and uphold rules for safety.

Qualified adults should supervise any team sport or activity that your child participates in. Select leagues and teams that have a commitment to safety and injury prevention. The team coach should have training in first aid and CPR. And don't take for granted that the coach enforces playing rules and requires that safety equipment be used at all times. See for yourself the level of competence at the management level. A coach with great training skills and confidence in his expertise will welcome your presence. Coaches should require and instruct youngsters on proper warm-ups and cooldowns.

4) Prepare your child for sport.

As we've mentioned several times before in this book, proper training and conditioning ensure a better chance of avoiding injury. Make sure the child has been adequately prepared with warm-ups and training sessions and that she is aware of her physical and mental strengths and weaknesses.

STEPS FOR INJURY PREVENTION

Encourage your child to follow these guidelines for the full enjoyment of his sport:

- Trust body cues (an unusual pain or soreness).
- Listen when your child says, "I'm tired."
- Encourage your child to take rest days.
- Vary the intensity of workouts.
- Visit the right specialists for fitness and nutrition consultation.

Q&A WITH DR. SMALL

Q *The coach of my son's little league team is pushing for my son, the team's star pitcher, to return to play after only two weeks' rest from an elbow injury. My son is nagging us to allow him to return, as the coach wishes. When do you think he can return?*

A Before your son returns to the lineup, he needs to be throwing for three to four days straight without pain. If he is, in fact, pain free, you can be more comfortable with his return to his place on the team.

Q *My thirteen-year-old daughter was just diagnosed with spondylolysis (stress fracture of the lower back). I am afraid she might suffer complications from this injury as she ages. What do you suggest to make her recovery most successful?*

A Believe it or not, stress fractures of the lower back are quite common in hyperextension sports, such as gymnastics, figure skating, and dance. The treatment is physical therapy, directed at strengthening the abdominal muscles and hip flexor muscles, as well as improving the flexibility of the hamstrings. In addition, a rigid back brace is usually required for a period of three to nine months, worn up to twenty-three hours a day.

If the treatment protocol is not followed, this type of stress fracture may not heal and will eventually lead to one vertebra moving out of alignment. By the time the condition gets to this point, it is irreversible. The child who receives no treatment may grow up to become an adult with constant, severe back pain.

Q My son suffered a concussion last week after colliding with another player during soccer practice. He still has head pain but wants to play in today's game. Can he play?

A A child cannot return to contact sports if he is suffering from any residual neurological symptoms. These symptoms include headaches, blurred vision, and nausea. If he still has any of these symptoms, your son must see a doctor. Your son must be fully symptom-free for at least a week before returning to play. If a child returns to play while still symptomatic and then receives another trauma or blow on the head, severe injury or possibly even death may result because of residual swelling and pressure on the brain.

Q My son was knocked unconscious during a football game. He regained consciousness and returned to his game. Does he need to see a physician?

A Your son most definitely needs to see a physician within six to twelve hours. But if he has severe vomiting or severe headache or upper and lower body weakness, then he needs to see a physician immediately. When your son is symptom-free for a week, then he can return to play. Your son should not have returned to the game. After any child loses consciousness, he should wait a week before returning to contact sports.

Q What is the role of non-steroidal anti-inflammatory drugs (NSAID) in acute and chronic sports injuries?

A NSAIDs include ibuprofen and other related medications. In an acute injury, the NSAIDs can be used to manage pain and swelling. NSAIDs have both analgesic (anti-pain) and anti-inflammatory effects. If there is an acute injury, then the medication needs to be taken for one to two weeks on a daily basis. In certain sports where the level of playing is high, kids will often compete in pain and will take an analgesic when competing. But NSAIDs should not be used under these circumstances because the injury could then get worse.

Q My daughter runs track. What can we do to make sure she does not get injured and suffer from a common sports injury?

A Generally, a month or more before the sports season begins, she should begin to build up a run of thirty to sixty minutes at least three times per week. This simple plan is actually a primary prevention. If your daughter experiences any pain for up to one to two weeks, she should decrease her running mileage by 50 percent or more. When the pain disappears, your daughter can slowly build up her running by increasing the mileage by 10 to 20 percent a week, until she is back to her usual run.

Q My daughter and three other gymnastics teammates had stress fractures in their legs and feet this summer. Could these injuries have been prevented?

A If four girls had stress fractures in their legs and feet in the same time period, then something was probably amiss in their training. They may have been doing too much of one type of activity, such as floor exercises or vaulting. Done to excess, these impact activities would cause a stress fracture. Also, the girls may have been practicing on a harder surface than usual. Finally, they may have increased their number of hours of training over the summer by too many hours. If there is a specific injury pattern that you suspect might be the result of improper training, then speak with the coach to try and prevent similar occurrences in the future.

Q My son has Osgood-Schlatter Disease. His physician says there's nothing he can do about it and has to give up sports for several months. Is this true?

A Osgood-Schlatter Disease is really not a disease; it is a "growing pain" where the patella tendon inserts into the tibial tubercle. These kids experience pain just below their knees. In some cases merely bending down or squatting causes severe pain, while in others pain only ensues after intense running and jumping. In the more mild cases no activity restriction is required. In the more severe form, a decrease in the amount of activity often is needed. It is unusual for the child to have to give up sports for several months. In mild, moderate, and severe cases, stretching the hamstrings three or four times per day and performing leg lifts every other day will help with the discomfort.

Q How should a parent treat "growing pains?"

A If you take your child to her doctor for a physical, and all other possibilities for the pain have been ruled out, the child can be given over-the-counter, non-steroidal anti-inflammatory medication at the dosage set by the doctor. All exercise should be carefully monitored during this period by the parents so as not to aggravate the existing problem.

Q Are there other conditions that mimic growing pains that should cause concern?

A Growing pains are transient and generally do not last for more than a week or two in any location. They produce no tenderness to the touch. A simple over-the-counter anti-inflammatory, taken before bedtime, usually eliminates the pain altogether.

Pain that accompanies swollen joints, lumps, and bumps not associated with injury could be symptomatic of more serious conditions, such as, juvenile arthritis, tumors, infection or, more rarely, leukemia.

More than 99 percent of the time, these symptoms very rarely lead to the diagnosis of a disease. Sharp pain that is present during an athletic activity could also be caused by a growth plate fracture. If not treated early, these fractures can lead to uneven limbs and chronic pain into adulthood.

Q *My child's Little League coach says to play through the pain or don't play at all. I know this is wrong, yet I don't want my child to miss out on playing the sport he loves. What should I do?*

A Your instincts are right, and your role and responsibility as a parent supersedes the word of the coach. I advise you to have a one-on-one conversation with this person and tell him that you want your child to enjoy the sport, but not at the cost of his health, nor damage to his body.

If the coach fails to see your point, have him take it up with your child's doctor. Your child should not be permanently removed from the team because he cannot play due to an injury.

Q *What will happen to my son who keeps spraining his ankle?*

A In the short run, your son will not be able to perform his normal activities to his fullest. He will often have swelling at the end of the day or after activity. In the long term, twenty years down the road, he may develop arthritis and severely restricted range of motion. I would advise a good rehabilitation/exercise program before he enters into competitive sports. It takes one to two months to see a significant improvement.

CHAPTER TWELVE

REHABILITATION FROM SPORTS INJURIES

Twelve-year-old Max dislocated his shoulder while playing basketball. After the injury, he went to see his pediatrician. The pediatrician recommended ibuprofen, ice, and rest for a few weeks. But after a week, Max's shoulder became worse. It was now stiff, weak, and more painful than before.

At this point, Max and his parents came to see me. I told them the pain and stiffness was typical of all athletes who are injured and don't properly rehab their injury. In order to return to competition, Max needed to follow a four-step plan to regain his strength, range of motion, and sport-specific skills. After a few weeks of following his prescribed rehab plan, he was back at his game.

Generally, an athlete who has been injured and out of competition for a certain length of time will need, with rehabilitation, half that original length of time to get back into play. For example, if your child has been out of competition and sports for four weeks, she will need approximately two weeks of rehabilitation. Seeking professional help immediately is important—early therapy will prevent internal scar tissue, and your athletic youngster can anticipate a quicker and more complete recovery and an earlier return to competition.

Exercises that are prescribed by your child's physician are done with a *Physical Therapist* (PT) and can be done in the therapist's office on an ongoing basis, two to three times a week for one to two months. If the injury is not too severe, a physical therapist may give your child a home exercise program.

An *Athletic Trainer* might also be assisting your child in a school setting. The difference between a physical therapist and an athletic trainer is in their schooling. An athletic trainer is more geared toward first aid and immediate management of sports injuries but is quite capable of providing exercises. A physical therapist is not required to be trained in first aid (though many are); rather, the physical therapist's focus is on rehabilitation exercises. Both the physical therapist and the athletic trainer will use various methods to control pain and inflammation, such as ice, ultrasound, and electronic stimulation.

But before your child can return to play, she must progress through the following stages of rehabilitation.

STAGE ONE: EARLY MOBILIZATION AND RESTORATION OF RANGE OF MOTION (ROM)

The goal of Stage One is to decrease your child's pain and inflammation, and to begin to reestablish your child's former range of motion. It is essential for your child to begin range of motion exercises and light aerobic exercise (biking, swimming, or other nonimpact activities) as soon as possible.

Even if the injured area is somewhat tender, early mobilization helps to combat disabling swelling and muscle atrophy and minimize the loss of range of motion in the joint. A small degree of soreness is generally acceptable, but more acute pain is an indication that your child must hold back and reduce the level of activity. For moderate to severe injury, anti-inflammatory medication might be used to control swelling and pain. This should be discussed with your child's physician.

Your child's medical team may use various *therapeutic modalities* in Stage One of the recovery. The term "therapeutic modality" refers to any of the various techniques that a physician, physical therapist, or athletic trainer employs to decrease swelling, pain, and inflammation and expedite the healing process. Therapeutic modalities used in Stage One include: ultrasound (a machine that carries sound waves and helps stimulate blood flow to injured area), electronic stimulation (a machine that applies electrical pulses to increase blood flow to injured area), icing, and whirlpool. These are used to stimulate blood flow and repair damaged tissue, which lessens pain and swelling. In addition, with these modalities, nonimpact activities such as swimming and biking are important to keep the muscles moving.

STAGE TWO: STRENGTH, BALANCE, AND FLEXIBILITY TRAINING

The goal in Stage Two of rehabilitation is to achieve almost full strength and a complete range of motion. In this stage, the athlete begins a progressive resistance program.

Your child will continue to use the modalities begun in Stage One, but now the rehabilitation team will be aggressively adding exercises to improve your child's strength, balance, and function. Exercise frequency is increased to several times a day. Though therapy often focuses on one particular muscle group, it is now necessary that the complementary muscles be strengthened as well. For example, if your child hurt her shoulder, in Stage One she would be doing arm lifts without weights. In Stage Two she would be doing the same arm lifts, but now it would be with weights, and the arm would be moving in three to four different directions.

Sample Stage Two Exercises For An Ankle Sprain Include:

- *Resistance band exercises in an up/down, in/out motion.* We begin with one set of ten, one time a day, and gradually increase to six sets of ten, two to three times a day. (See Figure 37, page 174.)

- *Toe raisers* (standing on the edge of a stair, raising up on the toes as far as you can, then lowering the heels down as far as possible). Starting at one set of five, one time a day, to six sets of ten, two to three times a day. (See Figure 38, page 175.)
- *Balance exercises—One-legged balance drills.* An athlete stands on the injured leg and tosses a medicine ball or basketball to a partner ten to fifteen times in rapid succession. This drill is done on a flat surface or standing on a trampoline. (See Figures 48-50, pages 182-183.)
- *Standing on a waffle board* (a flat disc with a ball on the bottom) to improve balance.

STAGE THREE: SPORT-SPECIFIC TRAINING

The goal of Stage Three is to have the athlete perform well with sport-specific tasks. Different sports require using various motor skills and muscle strength. Sport-specific training is the marriage of basic strength, balance, and flexibility training with sport-specific activities in order to reeducate the muscles to perform the necessary movements needed for a particular sport.

Once your child demonstrates that he can perform sport-specific skills in practice, participation in the sport can be resumed—with proper precautions. The intensity of the athlete's exercise also picks up at this point. Functional success in these exercises is generally the last hurdle before your child can return to full competition.

Sport-specific skills for a running sport include running, cutting (changing directions at various speeds), and jumping:

- Intense running is resumed and cardiovascular fitness and muscle endurance is rebuilt using a skiing machine, bike, stair, stepping machine, or a treadmill.
- Agility drills are begun by running figure eights and running zigzag patterns. (See Figure 18, page 164.)

- More intense balance and strength exercises are added, such as hopping and jumping. These activities are called *plyometrics*. (See Figure 16, page 163.)

For an upper-body sport, activities include:

- Light tosses from three to five feet.
- Various passing movements, two-handed and one-handed, with a basketball or a soccer ball.
- More intense balance and strength exercises, such as throwing a ball against a backboard, for longer distances and with more intensity.

STAGE FOUR: MAINTENANCE

The goal of Stage Four is to improve upon the athlete's strength and sport-specific skills, so the injured body part is stronger and more functional than prior to the injury.

Injured athletes should continue to do a home exercise program. Now is also the time to increase strength, balance, and flexibility in the training program. There are no new exercises given at this point. Remember, the Stage Four exercises constitute a maintenance program. Your child will continue to do the same specific exercises for three to six months in order to prevent a reoccurrence of the injury. This maintenance program usually involves continuing to increase repetitions and weights on the various exercises.

The following suggested rehab program should be done only under the guidance of a physician and carried out with a professional physical therapist. (See Chapter Thirteen for more detailed explanations and diagrams for these exercises.)

ACUTE INJURIES				
	Ankle Sprain	Hip Flexor Injury	Shoulder Dislocation	Patella Dislocation
Missed Time	2–8 weeks	3–12 weeks	4–12 weeks	4–12 weeks
Stage I	Icing, ultrasound for stimulation; range of foot motion—up/down/in/out; toe raisers; stationary biking as soon as possible	Gentle stretching and ROM; stationary biking as soon as possible	Light ROM, not above head; pendulum exercises	Will be in knee immobilizer 4–6 weeks; do leg lifts and isometric exercises (no bending knee)
Stage II	Biking; advance to treadmill, resistance band exercises, calf stretches, one-legged balance drills, cutting drills	Leg lifts, hurdler's stretch, stationary biking, and walking on treadmill	Resistance band exercises, free weights, arm raisers	Begin ROM, straight leg raising with weights, progress as tolerated, one-legged balance drills
Stage III	Running on treadmill, running outside on padded surface, kicking, jumping, soccer, basketball, and tennis drills	Running on treadmill; running, kicking, and jumping; soccer, basketball, and tennis drills	Throwing balls, tennis serves	Progress walking and running on treadmill, start jumping and cutting drills, start sport-specific skills
Stage IV	Continue resistance band exercises and balance drills before and after sports	Continue leg lifts; continue stretches 3–4 times	Continue resistance band exercises, free weights	Continue leg lifts, wall squats

	Ankle Sprain	Hip Flexor Injury	Shoulder Dislocation	Patella Dislocation
Protective Equipment/ Bracing*	Crutches only for several days; it is extremely rare to have to cast an ankle sprain; in severe cases I prefer a walking boot. Ankle strap/brace.	None	Sling for comfort (ideally less than 7 days)	Knee immobilizer and crutches for 4-6 weeks; protective Neoprene knee brace with patella cut-out once out of immobilizer

CHRONIC / OVERUSE INJURIES				
	Shin Splints	Shoulder Tendonitis	Sever's Disease	Osgood-Schlatter Disease
Missed or Decreased Time	No running for 2–6 weeks	2-12 weeks	1–6 weeks	1–6 months
Stage I	Calf stretching, stationary biking, swimming, running in water	Decrease swimming, tennis serving, baseball, or pitching by 50 percent	Calf stretching 4 times per day, toe raisers, swimming, biking	Icing the tender bone, biking
Stage II	Resistance bands, toe raisers, toe walking/heel walking, one-legged balance drills;	Upper extremity stretching, internal and external rotation and arm raisers;	One-legged balance drills, towel scrunches,	Leg lifts in 3 directions

*The equipment is not the treatment; it is used as an adjunct. The primary treatment is the rehabilitation (therapy).

	Shin Splints	Shoulder Tendonitis	Sever's Disease	Osgood-Schlatter Disease
Stage II (continued)	begin walking on treadmill and progress to speed walking, and then running	after 1–2 weeks proceed to arm raisers	walking progressing to running	
Stage III	Add more bands, toe raisers, and stretches; progress to running	Add 10–20 percent per week for swimming, pitching, tennis serving; continue internal rotation, external rotation, and arm raisers	Cutting, jumping, kicking, and other sport-specific skills	Add 10–20 percent per week
Stage IV	Continue toe raisers, calf stretches	Continue at least 2 of 4 exercises	Continue calf stretches and resistance band	Continue stretches and leg lifts
Bracing, Orthotics, Other Equipment*	Over-the-counter orthotics; only if there is no response to rehab would you get the custom-made orthotics	None	Heel cushions, heel lifts, or over-the-counter orthotics	Osgood-Schlatter band; Neoprene knee sleeve with patella cut-out

Q&A WITH DR. SMALL

Q My seven-year-old daughter is complaining about pain in her lower back. She seems fine except when she runs. Her pediatrician says that regular activity will "work out" the pain. Does she need rehab?

A Most children after an injury, such as a sprain, fracture, or ligament pull, need some form of rehabilitation. It can be formal physical therapy or simple exercises to work the muscles into a strengthened position. Your injured child needs to see a doctor who can diagnose the painful area and recommend an exercise routine. Without exercise, a painful muscle can turn into a more serious and painful condition.

Q A doctor says that our son must have arthroscopic knee surgery. Are there any alternatives to the knee surgery?

A Before surgery, you should consider a rehab program for your child. Often, this will cure the situation or significantly alleviate the symptoms. If your son does need surgery, the physical therapy program will get him on the road to recovery that much faster. And remember: Always get a second opinion before surgery.

Q Are there such things as a pediatric physical therapist?

A Yes there are. A pediatric physical therapist is someone who specializes in treating children. They generally are very perky and enthusiastic, and most often have special training in pediatric physical therapy.

Q What should I look for in a rehab facility?

A There are several things to look for: (1) Look for a low patient to therapist ratio. Some facilities work with five or more patients at a time. Rather, look for a facility that works one-on-one. (2) The facility and staff should be child-friendly and upbeat. (3) The therapists should be open to your comments, and allow you, the parent, to take an active role in your child's therapy.

Q *My son has a broken leg. He'll be in a cast for eight weeks. Will he need physical therapy, and, if so, for how long?*

A He will indeed need physical therapy. When he comes out of the cast, he will have lost significant muscle strength, balance, and range of motion. It is important not to return your youngster back to competitive sports without this therapy. If your child returns to competition too soon, he would be at significant risk of suffering another injury to his ankle or knee because of his weak leg.

As for how long your son needs to be in therapy, follow the general guideline: Therapy should last for about half the amount of time your son was immobilized. Since your son has been in a cast for eight weeks, he will need approximately four weeks of therapy.

Q *My son sprained his ankle, and our local physical therapist does not accept our insurance. What should I do?*

A There are several things for you to do. First, you can pay out of your pocket and try to negotiate directly with the physical therapist for a discounted rate. Second, you can go for one or two visits with the therapist and work with her to design a home exercise program. An athletic trainer at school can help with rehabilitation, too. Finally, your doctor can help develop a home rehab program if the other options do not work out.

Q *My daughter has been in physical therapy for two months and does not seem to be improving. As a matter of fact, she is getting worse. What do you think?*

A There should be considerable improvement in your daughter after one month of therapy. Since your daughter is getting worse, I suggest seeking the opinion of another doctor. The original diagnosis might have been wrong.

Q *I have a twelve-year-old daughter who is on the basketball team. Many of them wear knee braces. Will these prevent injuries? Do you recommend them?*

A Prophylactic knee bracing is not recommended, nor do they prevent injury. In fact, if an injury occurs with the knee brace, it could be worse than without the knee brace. I only recommend knee braces for specific conditions: after ligament injuries, patella tendonitis, Osgood-Schlatter, after patella dislocation, and patellafemoral pain syndrome.

Q *My daughter is ten years old, and she has had eight ankle sprains in the last two years. Her first injury was treated with two weeks of crutch walking, after which she reinjured herself. Will she benefit from physical therapy?*

A Therapy will absolutely help her. I'm sure her muscle strength and balance are significantly altered. Once she feels better, she needs to do at least five to ten minutes of ankle exercises for as long as she plays sports; hopefully this will be for the rest of her life.

Q *My son is a twelve-year-old tennis player and has had unrelenting shoulder pain for six months. He was told he has "shoulder tendonitis." He had one month of physical therapy, which seemed to help a bit. He is still having pain, accompanied by the sensation that his shoulder "pops" out of joint. His doctors are telling us there is nothing more that can be done; he must give up tennis. What do you think?*

A Your son may have shoulder tendonitis, but he also likely has an unstable shoulder—the muscles at the front of the shoulder are very strong, while the muscles at the back of the shoulder and upper back are weak. Every time he serves or hits an overhead, his shoulder jerks forward partially out-of-socket and causes pain. I would recommend another month of appropriate physical therapy and then ongoing exercises for at least six months. With this plan, your child should be relatively pain-free and be able to play competitive tennis.

CHAPTER THIRTEEN

FLEXIBILITY, STRENGTH, AND CONDITIONING

Twelve-year-old Rob often complained of muscle soreness and spasms when he came home from soccer practice. His coaches said these spasms were due to tight muscles. For example, when Rob tried to touch his toes, he could only reach his fingertips a third of the way to the ground, while other stretches brought pain to his shoulders, torso, and hamstrings.

Although Rob was considered a talented soccer player, his coach explained his need to become more flexible, and suggested that he undertake some flexibility training. "If you could become more flexible," he explained to Rob, "you could become a more explosive player."

With an appropriate and interesting workout, Rob's spasms are now gone and pain is no longer an issue. Rob is scoring more goals and feeling a lot more confident about his skills.

YOUR CHILD'S STRENGTHS AND WEAKNESSES

Every parent wants to know: "How can my child become a better player or athlete?" The answer lies in your child's physical strengths and weaknesses.

Some kids are naturally quick and agile but these kids may need (1) **muscle strengthening** to make them better athletes. Other kids are strong and powerful, yet they may lack quickness and agility and therefore need (2) **agility training.** Some children are tight in their muscles and consequently need a (3) **flexibility program.** Finally, there are young athletes who are quick, agile, and flexible but lack stamina and need (4) **endurance training, or aerobic training.**

The following recommendations are for kids ages ten and older, and are designed to improve their strength, agility, flexibility, and endurance in order to improve performance and protect against injury. Most children under the age of ten lack the discipline to perform the exercises on a regular basis. By building up weaker physical areas, your child will round out her skill level and thereby become a better, more confident player.

WORKOUT ONE: GENERAL WORKOUT TO IMPROVE OVERALL MUSCLE STRENGTH*

Exercise	Repetitions	Starting Weight (pounds)	Example
Bench Press	3 sets of 10	50	Fig. 5, p.158
Lat Pull-down	3 sets of 10	10–20	Fig. 6, p.158
Biceps	3 sets of 10	10	Fig. 7, p.158
Triceps	3 sets of 10	5	Fig. 8, p.158
Knee Extension	3 sets of 10	50	Fig. 13, p.161
Knee Flexion	3 sets of 10	30	Fig. 14, p.161

* The starting weight should be a weight that is not too easy and not too hard to lift. It should be a challenge to lift the weight at the ninth and tenth repetitions.

Workout for Upper Body Sports

When your young athlete uses many overhand movements, in sports such as tennis, swimming, and baseball, a suitable workout plan goes like this:

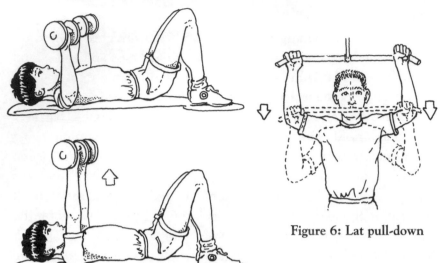

Figure 6: Lat pull-down

Figure 5: Bench press

Figure 7: Bicep curl

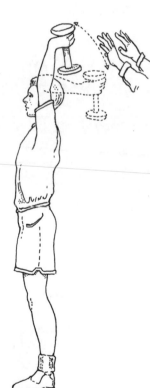

Figure 8: Tricep extension

- Aerobic warm-up for five to ten minutes
- Flexibility exercises for two to five minutes
- Upper body muscle strengthening (bench press, lat pull down, rows, and arm raisers) using free weights, resistance bands, and medicine balls
- Aerobic training for twenty to thirty minutes
- Cooldown exercises
- Finally, repeat another set of flexibility exercises

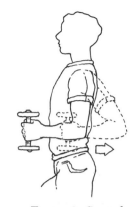

Figure 9: Seated or standing rows

Specific Exercises	Repetitions	Starting Weight (in Pounds)	Example
Bench Press	3 sets of 10	50	Fig. 5, p.158
Lat Pull-down	3 sets of 10	10–20	Fig. 6, p.158
Seated or Standing Rows	3 sets of 10	5–10	Fig. 9, p.159
Arm Raisers	3 sets of 10	3	Fig. 23, p.168

Workout for Lower Body Sports

When your young athlete's sport requires a great deal of running, such as track, lacrosse, soccer, and field hockey, the following plan is recommended:

- Aerobic warm-up for five to ten minutes
- Flexibility exercises for two to five minutes
- Lower body muscle-strengthening exercises (leg lifts, knee extension, and flexion) for twenty to thirty minutes
- Specific aerobic exercises, such as running and cycling, for twenty to thirty minutes
- Cooldown exercises
- Finally, repeat another set of flexibility exercises

Exercise	Repetitions	Starting Weight (pounds)	Examples
Leg Lifts	3 sets of 10	2 pounds; increase to 10 pounds over 2–3 months	Figs. 34-36, p. 173-174
Isometric Quad Sets	1 set of 10	No weight	Fig. 10, p.160
Lunges*	1 set of 5	No weight	Fig. 11, p.160
Squats*	1 set of 5	No weight	Fig. 12, p.161
Knee Extension	3 sets of 10	50	Fig. 13, p.161
Knee Flexion	3 sets of 10	30	Fig. 14, p.161

*I do not recommend these exercises until age fifteen or sixteen, as they are hard to master. Oftentimes the youngsters bend their knees too much, which may cause knee or back injury.

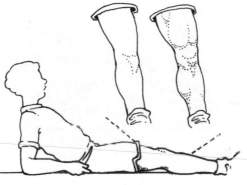

Tighten quad muscles without moving leg for 15-20 seconds. Release and repeat.

Figure 10: Isometric quad sets

Do not bend front knee beyond toes.

Figure 11: Lunges

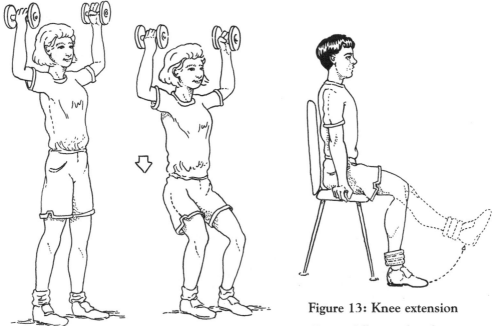

Figure 12: Squats

Do not bend knees beyond toes.
Keep back straight.

Figure 13: Knee extension

Do not fully straighten legs.

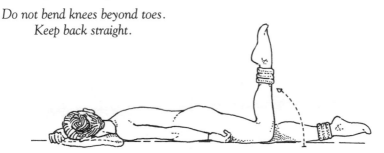

Figure 14: Knee flexion
Do not fully bend (flex) knee.

WORKOUT TWO: AGILITY TRAINING WORKOUT TO IMPROVE AGILITY, SPEED, AND QUICKNESS

It is important to explain speed, agility, and quickness. Speed is the ability or the time it takes to move from point A to B. Agility and quickness are related to movement, too, but they deal with reflexes and reaction time. One could be fast but not quick, or quick but not fast. Quickness and agility are especially important in lateral move-ment in sports such as tennis, soccer, basketball, hockey, football, and cutting sports (sports that involve a lateral movement, a quick change of direction—such as Ultimate Frisbee or field hockey).

Help your child pick two or three of these drills to do one to two times per week. They should be performed two or three days apart. If the exercises are done on consecutive days there is a high chance of knee, shin, or ankle injury and a stress fracture.

Box Drills

- Drill 1: Draw a box on the ground, and divide the box into areas I, II, III, IV. Count how many seconds it takes to jump around the box. Do this with two legs, right-legged, and left-legged.
- Drill 2: Do Drill 1 with a partner, for ten to thirty seconds. Then call out two numbers from the grid. (See Figure 15 below). Do this three or four times. Finally call out three numbers and jump to the different boxes.

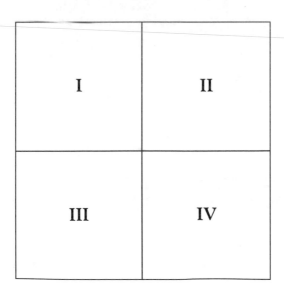

Figure 15: Box drill

Jumping Drill

- Practice jumping off of and onto boxes. Purchase two, three, and five feet plyo boxes. A plyo box is a platform with a sturdy, flat base and top. Athletes jump onto and off of the box to improve their jumping ability, power, and explosiveness. These can be purchased through websites and catalogues that deal with training and running. This method of jumping and movement training is called plyometrics.

Figure 16: Plyometric drills

Whistle Drill

- Sprint forward, backward, and shuffle sideways, changing direction every time the whistle blows.

Agility Ladder Drill

- An agility ladder is a rope ladder that is placed on the ground. Athletes run through the ladder—forward, backward, sideways—trying not to hit the rope or rungs. This is similar to football players running through tires. The agility ladder helps develop foot quickness and coordination.

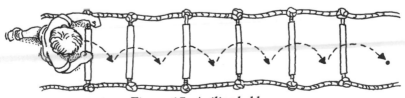

Figure 17: Agility ladder

Figure of Eight Drill

- In this drill, the youngster runs in a zigzag or figure of eight pattern. Start at one cone, and run to the other cone. Stop for 1-2 seconds, shift weight to left foot, and then circle cone to the right. Repeat ten times. This will improve the child's agility, explosiveness, and speed.

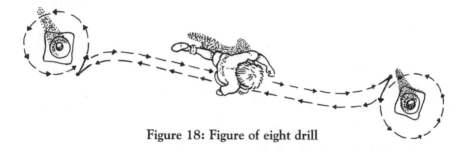

Figure 18: Figure of eight drill

WORKOUT THREE: FLEXIBILITY TRAINING WORKOUT

Some athletes are so inflexible that they can't even touch their toes! Adequate flexibility is important—loose and elongated muscle works more efficiently and with more power because more of the muscle is at work. And a flexible muscle is less likely to cramp up and become injured.

How to Stretch

Most people think the best time to stretch is before exercise. However, a cold muscle should never be stretched because it could tear. Initially, a five-minute warm-up should precede the stretching period, and the absolute best time to stretch is after exercise, to prevent the muscles from tightening up.

The stretches that should be performed depend on the sport that the child is playing and what muscle groups he has used. In a running sport, the hamstrings or quadriceps should be stretched; in an upper body sport, the shoulders and upper back should be stretched.

To improve muscle range of motion, stretches (flexibility exercises) should be done four to five times per day, and before and after a sporting activity. Stretching one time per day or only two to three times per week will maintain flexibility but will not improve flexibility.

Young athletes often say they do not have the time to stretch four or five times per day. But when they are convinced that the stretching may improve their performance, they are more likely to comply. Most children brush their teeth in the morning and in the evening. I can generally convince them to stretch at these two times. It should not be too difficult to do the stretches another two times during the day (perhaps while waiting for the bus or at lunch time).

The three general areas to stretch are the quadriceps, the hamstrings, and the shoulders.

Quadriceps

- Lying on your stomach, bring your heel to your buttocks and hold for twenty seconds. Repeat with the other leg.

Figure 19: Quadriceps stretch

Hamstrings

- Place your foot on a bench or a chair and lean forward, keeping the heel of the other leg firmly to the ground. Hold for twenty seconds. Repeat with the other leg.

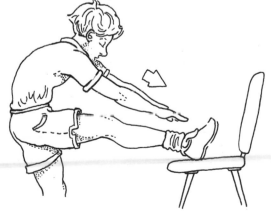

Figure 20: Hamstring stretch with foot on chair

Figure 21: Hands above head stretch

**Figure 22:
Towel stretch**
See page 176 for explanation.

Shoulder and Upper Back

- Hands above head stretch: Clasp your hands together and stretch them above your head, with the palms facing up. Hold for twenty seconds.

WORKOUT FOUR: WORKOUT TO IMPROVE AEROBIC ENDURANCE

Endurance or stamina is important in soccer, basketball, tennis, and many other sports. Young athletes need to be able to perform as well at the beginning of the game or competition as they do at the end. If the child is tired out toward the end, she obviously will not be performing up to potential.

To improve one's aerobic endurance or stamina, it is necessary to perform continuous activity (biking, swimming, running, skiing, etc.) for at least twenty minutes, two to three times per week. Pick a time or a distance one is comfortable with—e.g., one mile or fifteen minutes. Do this two to three times per week. Increase the distance or the time by 10 percent every two weeks. A minimum goal would be forty-five to sixty minutes, three times per week.

PREVENTIVE EXERCISES

Parents and coaches often ask if there are any preventative exercises that a child can do to prevent injury and possibly improve performance. The answer lies in the exercises outlined below. Different sports use different muscles. There are certain injury patterns that occur in different sports. For example, in baseball, tennis, and swimming, injuries of the shoulder commonly occur (shoulder subluxation/shoulder tendonitis). In running sports—lacrosse, soccer, field hockey, track, and cross-country running—knee, ankle, and foot injuries commonly occur. If your child is serious about his sport and is practicing three or more times per week, it would be appropriate for him to do the recommended exercises.

RECOMMENDED STRENGTHENING EXERCISES TO PRE-VENT SPORTS INJURY AND IMPROVE PERFORMANCE

Shoulder (baseball, tennis, swimming)

1. Arm Raisers
2. Internal Rotation
3. External Rotation

Start with a three-pound weight. Perform three sets of ten. Every two weeks increase by a set of ten to get up to six sets of ten. At that point increase the weight by one or two pounds and begin at three sets of ten.

Arm Raisers: The arms should be placed 30–45 degrees in front of the shoulder and lifted up to shoulder level. (See Figure 23, page 168.) The thumbs should be pointed downward.

Internal Rotation: The youngster should lie on his back and place

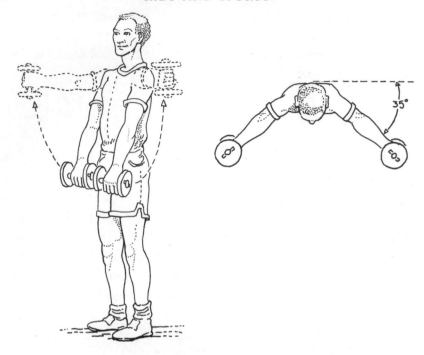

Figure 23: Arm raiser

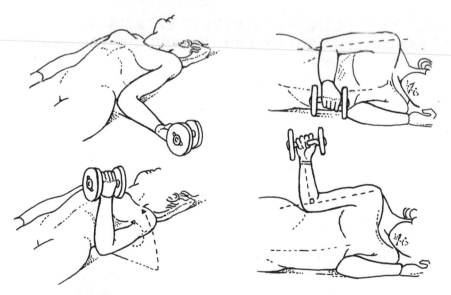

Figure 24: Shoulder
internal rotation

Figure 25: Shoulder
external rotation

elbow at side. The lower arm should be at a 90 degree angle with the upper arm. (See Figure 24, page 168.)

External Rotation: The youngster should lie on her side and place elbow at side. The lower arm should be at a 90 degree angle with the upper arm. (See Figure 25, page 168.)

Elbow/Wrist (gymnastics, baseball, tennis)

1. Wrist Extension
   Have arm resting on thigh with palm down.
2. Wrist Flexion
   Have arm resting on thigh with palm up.

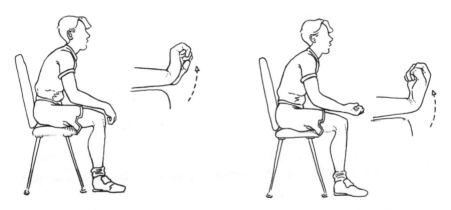

Figure 26: Wrist extension   Figure 27: Wrist flexion

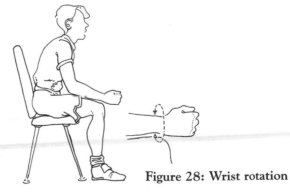

Figure 28: Wrist rotation

3. Wrist Rotation

Have arm resting on side with palm down. Rotate to outside of body and then toward the inside.

Begin with one pound and perform three sets of ten. Every two weeks increase by a set of ten to get up to six sets of ten. At that point one can increase to two pounds and do three sets of ten.

Low Back (tennis, gymnastics, figure skating, dance)

1. Abdominal Crunch

Lie on back, knees bent, and hands behind the head. Raise head and upper back one third of the way off the ground. Hold for five seconds. Start out with one set of ten and work up to three sets of fifty. (See Figure 1, page 123.)

2. Pelvic Tilt/Bridging

Place low back/buttocks into the air and hold for twenty seconds. Get into abdominal crunch position—bent knees and hands behind head. Lift mid and lower back one third of the way off the ground and hold for five seconds. (See below.)

3. Pointer Stretch

Lift right arm/left leg parallel to the ground and in alignment with shoulder and hip. Hold for twenty seconds and repeat five to ten times. Then lift left arm and right leg. (See Figure 30, page 171.)

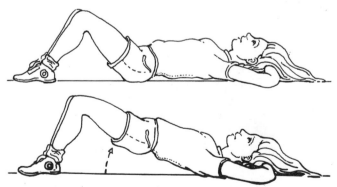

Figure 29: Pelvic tilt/Bridging

Figure 30: Pointer stretch

4. Rocking Back and Forth

   Get into abdominal crunch position—bent knees and hands behind head. Rotate knees to left side and then to right side trying to touch knees to ground. Hold for five seconds. Perform twenty to twenty-five times. (See below.)

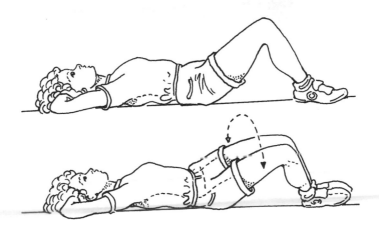

Figure 31: Rocking back and forth

5. Knees to Chest

Get into abdominal crunch position—bent knees and hands behind head. Bring both knees to chest and hold for twenty seconds. Repeat two times, two-legged and then one-legged.

Figure 32: Knees to chest

6. Camel/Cat

Lift belly up toward sky and form a hump. Place belly downward and create an indentation in mid/lower back. Go up and down fifteen to twenty times. Hold for five seconds.

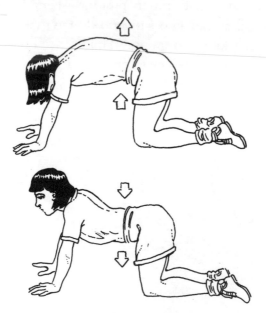

Figure 33: Camel/Cat
Hold each position for five seconds.

Knee (track, soccer, basketball, field hockey, lacrosse, hockey)

Straight Leg Raising (leg lifts)

1. Straight Leg Raising (lying on back)
2. Straight Leg Raising (lying on side)
3. Straight Leg Raising (lying on stomach)

Lying on back: Have foot flexed, toes pointing toward head, with opposite knee bent. Lean on elbows so as not to create back pain. Perform three sets of ten three times per week; start with two pounds, and increase ½ pound every two weeks to get up to ten pounds.

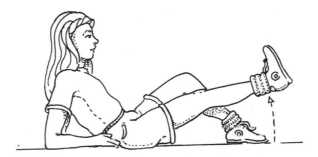

Figure 34: Straight leg raising—lying on back

Lying on side: Lie on side with bottom knee bent thirty to forty degrees. Have ankle/foot of upper leg in a neutral position. Lift leg up to shoulder height. Hold for five seconds. Perform three sets of ten

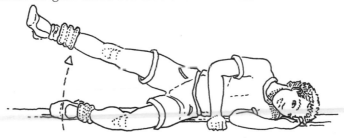

Figure 35: Straight leg raising—lying on side

three times per week; start with two pounds, and increase ½ pound every two weeks to get up to ten pounds.

Lying on stomach: Lie on stomach with feet in a comfortable position. Perform three sets of ten three times per week; start with two pounds, and increase ½ pound every two weeks to get up to ten pounds.

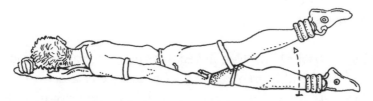

Figure 36: Straight leg raising—lying on stomach

If two pounds is too heavy, the youngster may start with zero, one, or one-and-a-half pounds.

Ankle (track, soccer, basketball, field hockey, lacrosse, hockey)

1. Resistance Band Exercises
   Place resistance band at ball of foot. Move ankle/foot in four directions (down, up, in, and out). Do three sets of ten.

2. Toe Raisers
   Place ball of foot on stairs. Bring heel above level of stair and then below level of stair. Perform three sets of ten—two-legged, and then one-legged. (See Figure 38, page 175.)

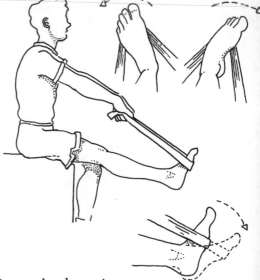

Figure 37: Ankle resistance band exercises

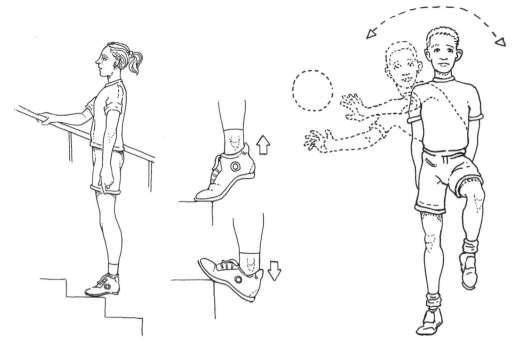

Figure 38: Toe raisers on stairs	**Figure 39:** **One-legged balance drill**

3. One-Legged Balance Drill
   Stand on one leg and have partner throw a medicine ball, basketball, or soccer ball ten to fifteen times to center of body, to right, and to left. (See above.)

Foot/Toe (soccer, dance, track, and figure skating)

1. Towel Scrunches
   Grab a towel, paper, or a washcloth with toes and then release. Perform two sets of twenty.
2. Writing Alphabet with Toes
   Write alphabet one to two times in script with an emphasis on moving the big toe. (See Figure 41, page 176.)

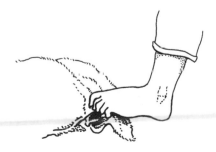

Figure 40: Towel scrunches

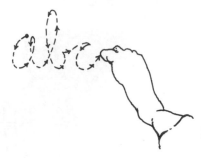

*Parents are encouraged to do these with their children. They may also do the exercises alone to prevent their own sports injuries!

Figure 41: Writing alphabet with toes

RECOMMENDED STRETCHES TO PREVENT SPORTS INJURY AND IMPROVE PERFORMANCE

Shoulder (baseball, tennis, gymnastics)

1. Hands Above Head Stretch
   Clasp hands together and place above head. Hold for twenty seconds; repeat twice before and after competition or practice. (See Figure 21, page 166.)
2. Towel Stretch/"Back Scratching"
   Place right hand above head and left hand in lower back. Grab a towel or a resistance band. Hold for twenty seconds; repeat twice before and after competition or practice. (See Figure 22, page 166.)

Wrist/Elbow (baseball and tennis)

1. Forearm Stretch
   Place palm/wrist in the upward direction with the elbow straight. Apply pressure with the opposite hand. Hold for twenty seconds; repeat before and after practice or competition.

Figure 42: Forearm stretch

Hip (track, soccer, gymnastics, figure skating)

1. Indian Style Stretch
   Sit down on floor with bent knees and feet placed together.

Figure 43: Indian style stretch

Figure 44: Hurdler style stretch

Apply downward pressure on knees with hands. Hold for twenty seconds; repeat before and after practice or competition.

2. Hurdler Style Stretch

This is similar to performing a lunge, but with the athlete holding the position. The feet should be 1½ to 2 shoulder-lengths apart. Place left foot in front of right. Place back knee twelve inches from the ground. Hold for twenty seconds. Do not bounce; repeat before and after practice or competition.

Knee (track, soccer, gymnastics, figure skating)

1. Quadriceps Stretch

Lie on ground, bend knee, and grab foot/ankle to buttocks. Hold for twenty seconds; repeat before and after practice or competition. (See Figure 19, page 165.)

2. Hamstring Stretch

Sit on ground with knees straight. Then bend knees to 15 to 20 degrees and lean forward. Hold for twenty seconds; repeat before and after practice or com-petition.

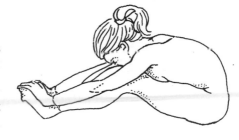

Figure 45: Hamstring stretch

Ankle/Heel (soccer, basketball, field hockey, lacrosse)

1. Wall Stretch (back knee straight)

   Place right foot six inches from wall and apply pressure to the back foot while keeping the back knee straight. Do not lift back heel off the ground. Hold for twenty seconds; repeat before and after practice or competition. This stretch works the upper part of the calf (gastrocnemius).

2. Wall Stretch (back knee bent)

   Place right foot six inches from wall and apply pressure to the back foot while bending the back knee. Do not lift the back heel off the ground. Hold for twenty seconds; repeat before and after practice or competition. This stretch works the lower part of the calf (soleus muscle) and Achilles tendon.

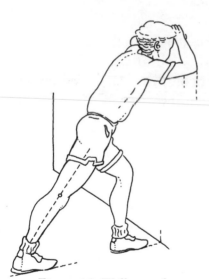 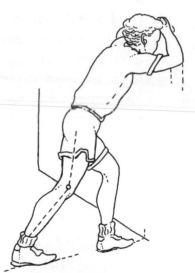

Figure 46: Wall stretch
(back knee straight)

Figure 47: Wall stretch
(back knee bent)

Q&A WITH DR. SMALL

Q My son is in ninth grade. He is gifted in basketball, but I noticed he lacks upper and lower body strength. It has been suggested that he work with weights, but he is not motivated. Can you make any suggestions?

A The answer to your question is not straightforward. You should definitely encourage your son, but don't push too hard, as that could turn him away. You may want to have the coach give him the appropriate exercises as a special assignment. The coach may encourage him to lead with the exercises while at practice. The coach can even assign the exercises to do at home with a teammate.

Q When is the best time to do stretching?

A The best time to stretch is after the muscles are warm. This is after a five- to ten-minute aerobic warm-up. The warm-up is especially critical on a cool day. It is also critical to end your workout or competition with stretching.

Q My child's coach says stretching is a waste of time. What do you think?

A There are two reasons to stretch. The first is to improve flexibility. Secondly, if your child is already flexible, she needs to maintain this flexibility. Many children who are going through a growth spurt have extremely tight muscles. It is particularly important for them to perform a stretching program. This includes doing simple stretches three to four times a day and holding these stretches for twenty seconds. For kids not going through a growth spurt, it's not as critical, but they should incorporate flexibility into their training program.

Q My daughter is on the club swim team. They swim five to six times per week, eleven months out of the year. They swim without strengthening or flexibility work. Don't they need to do something else besides swimming?

A To improve your daughter's swim time, it is important to cross-train, which in this case would be to do a workout on dry land. This cross-training workout could include resistance training, as well as flexibility training. Resistance training includes working with free weights and resistance bands. The flexibility training includes stretching for the upper and lower body. Such dry-land training is also important to prevent injuries, especially of the shoulders.

Q Should I buy bands or free weights to help with my daughter's resistance training program?

A It doesn't really matter. Bands are generally good for local muscle toning and muscle endurance. Free weights are generally better for improving general muscle strength. But if you're going on a trip, the bands are great because they are lightweight.

Q My son is trying to improve his stamina. He has been doing long runs two times per week for the past three weeks. When can he expect to improve his stamina?

A It may take anywhere from four to eight weeks to build up a training effect and to improve aerobic fitness. For your son to maintain his improved aerobic fitness, he needs to continue his running program or any aerobic sport for twelve to sixteen weeks, and for a minimum of two times per week.

Q How long will it take to build muscle strength?

A If your child were prepubertal, there would be marginal increases in muscle strength. If your child is in puberty, muscle strength and bulk will become more prominent. It takes at least four weeks to build up muscle strength.

Q *My son's coach recommended that he do weight training and stretches. But my son says he has no time for this. He tried the exercises for only about one week; the exercises take about twenty minutes to complete. What can we do?*

A A busy person can always find time to do these exercises. It is critical that you set up a schedule with your son to make this happen. No matter how old your child is, you can help him with time management. I often ask children with time-management problems, "Do you brush your teeth every night?" The child will answer yes. I then ask them to do only five minutes of the exercises before or after he brushes teeth.

Q *My son wants to improve his muscle strength. He has tried weights and resistance bands in the gym. He says they are boring. Is there anything else that he can do that is more interesting?*

A Working out with a friend can be helpful and certainly more interesting. A workout with medicine balls may be useful and enhance muscle strength. Here are some helpful examples:

Workout to Improve Muscle Strength and Endurance

Medicine Balls. A fun way to improve muscle strength and endurance is a medicine ball workout. Medicine balls are weighted balls that come in different weights (3 lb., 5 lb., 6 lb., 8 lb.). The workout can be completed with a partner or with a larger group. One should always start with the lightest weight, generally the 3 lb. ball, and should

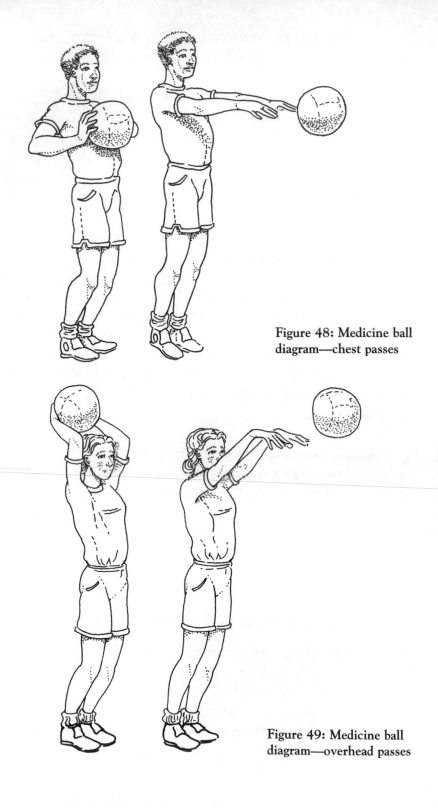

Figure 48: Medicine ball diagram—chest passes

Figure 49: Medicine ball diagram—overhead passes

Figure 50: Medicine ball diagram—twist passes

always rest one day between workouts to allow the muscles to heal. Start with the following sample workout:

10–15 chest passes
10–15 overhead passes
10–15 lateral rotation on right
10–15 lateral rotation on left

Q *Should children be doing different stretches than adults?*

A Both children and adults should be doing static stretches (holding the stretch for twenty seconds). Children should not be doing ballistic or dynamic stretches (a quick movement and stretch at the same time). There is a high risk for injury with such stretching. An example of a dynamic stretch would be bending repeatedly at the waist to touch the toes in an attempt to stretch the hamstrings. A better stretch would be to put a leg on a table and bend the body over the leg, holding this position for twenty seconds.

CHAPTER FOURTEEN

NUTRITIONAL GUIDANCE FOR THE ACTIVE CHILD

When Ryan first came to see me, he was a fourteen-year-old cross-country star who made the all-state team last season. At this point, he was even winning national meets in his age group. Yet, despite his competence in track and field, he complained to me that he was tired all the time. What struck me upon first glance was that he appeared too thin, even though runners are often quite lean. We discussed his medical history, during which he revealed that he also suffered from chronic muscle pain and headaches.

As we talked, these complaints disturbed me more than I let on. Ryan talked about very unusual symptoms for a high achiever, so I asked him what he was eating to keep up his strength. He reluctantly divulged that he read in a sports magazine that losing weight would give him more speed, so he cut his food intake to 1,200 calories per day, hoping that less weight on his already slim frame would improve his running times on the track. What had happened instead was muscle fatigue, which contributed to his constant aches and pains and chronic head pain. He also told me that his legs felt like Jell-O at the end of every day of training and competition. And Ryan's personality was suffering, too—his family, he complained, had begun to notice his cranky behavior.

Ryan had been skipping breakfast and eating only half a sandwich for lunch. He looked surprised at my evident concern and listened intently as I told him that he required 2,500 to 3,000 calories a day to maintain or improve his speed, and alleviate all his physical problems. I firmly advised him to eat five to six small meals a day and drink plenty of water. He asked me for examples of proper meals and snacks and appropriate drink selections while working out at the track, and I suggested pasta with cheese; a peanut butter and jelly sandwich; a turkey, chicken, or tuna salad sandwich; or yogurt and fruit.

FOOD: FRIEND OR FOE?

The truth is that although your athlete requires more calories than a sedentary person, optimum health is achieved through a balanced diet, and a balanced diet is managed with good nutrition. Sound nutritional and fitness habits developed during childhood have the potential to last a lifetime.

Every bit as important as the daily diet are the foods consumed prior to the athletic event, during competition, and after the game. For most athletic events, male and female athletes should consider the following:

Pregame Meals

Pregame meals should be eaten between one-and-one-half hours and three hours before the event. Yogurt with some granola and a banana, or a bagel with low-fat cheese or cream cheese makes a good pregame breakfast. A good pregame lunch or dinner could be pasta with chicken or cheese; a bean burrito with low-fat cheese, lettuce, and tomatoes; or some healthy combination of carbohydrates, proteins, and fats. Other good examples include a tuna, chicken, turkey, peanut butter and jelly, or grilled cheese sandwich plus yogurt and fruit. For vegetarians, a salad with low-fat cheese and bread, or pasta with tofu and vegetables is a healthy snack. Avoid high-fat sandwiches, such as burgers, hot dogs, and steak. Solid fat of this type is harder to digest and can cause dehydration when a meal containing them is followed by intense exercise.

Food During Competition

Small meals, such as a half sandwich, yogurt and fruit, energy bars, pretzels, or raisins can maintain energy during a workout and do not create problems of fullness that can lead to cramps. When a young athlete has an all-day tournament in sports such as gymnastics, soccer, or tennis, the family should develop a plan for packing healthy snacks. If the children don't bring their own food, their only choice becomes vending machine snacks like soda, chips, and candy bars.

Young athletes should be eating the "right stuff" every hour or two. The young athlete should not eat anything new, such as a spicy dish, the day of competition. The body functions best on small energy-packed food, such as half a sandwich, yogurt and fruit, or energy bars (a snack that has 200–300 calories with a combination of protein, carbohydrates, and fat). I can't emphasize the importance of healthy eating during a competition enough—children may spend as much as six to eight hours a day at a meet/competition. Obviously, if they haven't eaten for half a day, they cannot concentrate or perform at their best.

Postgame Meal

After competition, a dinner based on the food pyramid will rebuild strength and repair muscles that are challenged during competition. This means the meal should consist of complex carbohydrates, protein, and fats. It is at this point the child can have a high-fat meal if he desires. If burgers or pizza are on the athlete's mind, here is the perfect opportunity for the child to go to a fast-food chain without guilt.

Keep in mind that every child is different and needs a specific caloric intake calculated on body size, shape, and age, as well as the sports played. A high school swimmer, for instance, may require 5,000 to 6,000 calories a day! Balancing these calories is most important.

What sometimes conflicts with the need for large amounts of food is that our American diet, which relies on too many convenience foods, often does not consist of enough fruits and vegetables. Fruits and vegetables contain substances called antioxidants, which help prevent disease. An athlete at any level of performance needs large amounts of fruits and vegetables in order to repair muscles from injury or intense workouts, and boost immunity against even the common cold.

But even the healthiest diet is worthless if the child doesn't like to eat the foods a parent is offering. A parent should design a meal plan by taking into account the child's likes, dislikes, and preferences. Some children avoid all kinds of meat—any red meat, chicken, and turkey. One solution may be to "hide" the meat in casseroles, in salads, or in meat patties. Other children may have virtually no fruits or vegetables in their diet. If you have bowls and packages of fresh fruit on the kitchen or dining room table, your child will more likely eat them. Pack fruits or vegetables in your child's snack or lunch, especially during a competition. If it's there, she will definitely eat it. Always seek your child's input and vary the food selection.

THREE-DAY DIETARY RECALL

Whether your child is an elite athlete or overweight, it is important to see how many calories your child is ingesting. This gives us an idea if the child is overeating or lacks sufficient calories. Below is an example of a 12-year-old girl's Three-Day Dietary Recall, which is a recording of everything the athlete has had to eat and drink during a three-day period.

Sample Three-Day Dietary Recall

Breakfast:
½ cup Special K™ cereal
4 oz. nonfat milk
6 oz. orange juice
1 brewed tea (6 oz.), no sugar or milk

Snack:
1 Granny Smith apple

Lunch:
4 oz. grilled hamburger, 90 percent lean meat
1 Kaiser roll
2 tomato slices
Shredded lettuce
1 Diet Pepsi™
10 French fries
1 small tossed green salad with diet dressing

Dinner:
3 oz. beef stew with turnips, carrots, and spinach
10 oz. nonfat milk
1 low-fat dinner roll

Day Two

Breakfast:
½ cup Special K™ cereal with nonfat milk
6 oz. orange juice

Snack:
1 banana
1 slice American cheese

Lunch:
2 slices Swiss cheese on whole wheat
Lettuce and tomato
10 oz. nonfat milk
½ cup grapes
1 Diet Coke™

Dinner:
1 Uncle Ben's Rice Bowl™ (Teriyaki Chicken)
8 oz. nonfat milk
1 cup tossed salad with fat-free dressing

Day Three

Breakfast:
2 whole grain Eggo™ waffles
1 tbsp. maple syrup
6 oz. orange juice
½ cup pineapple

Snack:
1 oz. tortilla chips
¼ cup salsa

Lunch:
1 turkey sandwich on rye with lettuce, tomato, mustard
1 slice American cheese
1 oz. tortilla chips
10 mini-carrots
1 Diet Coke™

Dinner:
4 oz. grilled chicken breast
⅓ cup steamed white rice
½ cup steamed broccoli
8 oz. nonfat milk

> **Dietary Analysis of Day One**
>
> Total Calories: 1140
> Protein calories: 260 (23%)
> Carbohydrate calories: 580 (51%)
> Fat calories: 300 (26%)
>
> Important Nutrients
> Calcium: 660 mg.
> Iron: 12.8 mg.

The Three-Day Dietary Recall is an instructive exercise for the parent and child. Day One, for example, shows inadequate calories for growth, development, and sports participation or other physical activities. The diet is also low in calcium and iron. A child may need 2000-5000 calories each day, depending on how active they are (an athlete who trains up to three hours a day may need up to 5000 calories). Although the total calories are low, the analysis reveals a proper distribution of protein (which should be 20-30 percent), carbohydrates (50-60 percent), and fat (less than 30 percent).

IMPORTANT NUTRIENTS

There are many important nutrients that will keep your young athlete healthy and performing to the best of his ability. These are a few of the most vital; if your child is getting enough of these nutrients, chances are they're also getting enough of the rest.

Calcium

Calcium is an important mineral found in dairy products. Its main responsibility is to maintain heart, bone, and nervous system function. If consumption of calcium is too low, the bone density may be low and predispose the youngster to stress and hairline fractures. Optimum calcium intake from birth to age eight is 800 mg. per day. From ages eight to eighteen, children should ingest 1,300 mg. per day. Good sources of calcium include:

- Dairy products—milk, cheese, yogurt
- Green leafy vegetables—spinach, kale, collard greens
- Fish—salmon, especially with bones
- Bean curd (tofu)

Iron

Iron is an element that is important in the transport of oxygen through the cells. A deficiency of this element may lead to fatigue, concentration and memory lapses, and impaired athletic performances, especially in endurance sports (running, cycling, swimming, and skiing). Iron is generally found in:

- Red meat
- Green, leafy vegetables
- Dried fruit and legumes
- Dark meat of chicken and turkey

ARE YOU DRINKING ENOUGH?

Key to all body and athletic functioning is proper hydration. I am often questioned about the value of sports drinks as opposed to water. Sports drinks were designed for keeping energy levels high for sustained activity—sixty minutes or more of continuous exercise. With this long duration of intense movement, athletes naturally lose electrolytes, such as sodium and potassium.

I do recommend sports drinks for those children performing exercise of long duration. For all other types of exercise, water is probably good enough. The problem with tap or bottled water is that it has no taste, and children often won't drink enough of it. Therefore, I prefer that the young athlete drink flavored water or sports drinks over nothing at all. Sports drinks contain 5 to 6 percent carbohydrate (glucose or sugar). Apple juice and orange juice contain 10 to 12 percent carbohydrate. Any beverage containing more than 6 percent sugar that is consumed during competition may cause nausea and abdominal cramping in the athlete.

I suggest that if a child desires apple juice or any other high-sugar drink, the parent or coach should dilute the juice with the same amount of water. That way, you are giving the child no more glucose than that found in sports drinks.

Please keep this in mind when your child speaks of thirst: Children become dehydrated much faster than adults, and by the time they say they are thirsty, they are already dehydrated. This piece of information is especially important on hot, humid days. That's when dehydration can sneak up quickly on the young athlete. Make sure to encourage your child to drink eight ounces of fluid beyond his thirst level, thirty minutes prior to a sports activity. If game time is 10 A.M., coaches and parents should provide eight ounces of fluid at 9:30 A.M. Even if the child says he is not thirsty, insist that he drinks the fluid anyway. For every hour of play, a child should drink between eight and twelve ounces of fluid every half hour. Without water, the human body cannot function at its best.

If a coach, parent, and the young athlete are unaware of the threats from dehydration, vitamin and mineral deficiencies, and other disorders resulting from poor nutrition, the positives effects of athletics are left in the dust. By utilizing common sense and the suggestions above, a child can reduce the possibility of burnout, depression, social isolation, fatigue, and the desire to throw in the towel.

Advertising on television or in reading material gives children some information about fitness, but not all they need to make informed decisions. The best way to help them make proper decisions on their own is by example. Include your children, no matter how young, in decisions about nutritional purchases.

HOW TO MAKE IT ALL WORK
FOR YOU AND YOUR FAMILY

Good nutrition is a cumulative process, and athletes that only eat well on game days cannot expect to perform at their best. Here are some useful tips for you and your young athlete:

- Specific food planning for the day of an athletic competition requires that the family prepare specific snacks and drinks to bring to an event.
- Children must have breakfast every day, at a scheduled time. Breakfast is most vital on the day of a competition, and can include cereal with milk, fruit, and toast, or eggs with bread and fruit.
- Vary the items you serve before and during your child's athletic events. Serve your child's favorite health-conscious sandwiches one day and a macaroni and vegetable salad the next.
- Use unconventional breads for sandwiches, such as pita and bagels, and cut the sandwiches in shapes so that they are more appealing.
- Don't deny your children high-calorie snacks because they will certainly get them another way. A treat night should be scheduled one night per week, and of course on special occasions.
- Serve colorful vegetables in intriguing shapes with a tasty dip. Veggies pack a powerful nutritional punch, including vitamins, minerals, and fiber.
- Almost everyone likes fruit of some kind, so find out your child's favorites and serve them often.
- Most important: Set good examples for your children by eating the same foods you are encouraging them to eat.

Q&A WITH DR. SMALL

Q *My fourteen-year-old daughter competes in track at her school. Although she's got plenty of energy now, she's talking about becoming a vegetarian. Do you think this diet is OK for a growing girl?*

A First, let's define the concept of "vegetarianism." There are some vegetarians who eat no fish and no animal products of any sort, including products such as meat, milk, eggs, and cheese. Then there are those vegetarians who eat fish, eggs, and cheese but no meat. If one is very knowledgeable and meticulous in proper food selections, the vegetarian diet is safe enough for a young athlete, although it is extremely difficult to get enough calories and nutrients from being a strict vegetarian. More importantly, look at the number of calories a person is consuming and the percentage of the calories from protein. A young athlete should obtain 15 percent to 25 percent of total calories from protein.

In order to get proper nutrition, your daughter must mix certain imperfect foods to form a protein. Imperfect foods are products that, when combined with other foods, are a good source of protein. For example, she can combine rice with beans to form a protein. Another important element to keeping your daughter healthy is to supplement her diet with other protein sources, such as bean curd, soy milk, and other soy-based products.

I have found that it's extremely difficult for an active child to be a total vegetarian but not impossible. Look for any possible changes in your child's eating patterns and make suggestions as you go along.

Q *My ten-year-old son has hockey practice at 7 A.M. I can't get him to eat anything before he gets to the field. By the time practice ends at 8:30 A.M., he is already quite tired. His lunch at school isn't until 11 A.M. What can I do to get him to eat in the morning?*

A You have no choice but to get him to eat something thirty to sixty minutes before hockey practice. This does not have to be a huge breakfast—a small meal will suffice. Offer him a piece of bread with cheese, an egg (hardboiled or sunny-side up), yogurt with a piece of fruit, or cereal with milk and fruit. Have your son make the choice of foods, but tell him frankly that he cannot go to practice without eating—and don't give in. Eventually, eating a small breakfast will become part of the routine.

Q My fourteen-year-old son is very athletic and plays multiple sports, including basketball, soccer, and baseball. Coaches are constantly telling him that he needs to gain weight and "bulk up." No matter what he eats, he can't gain weight. Do you have any suggestions?

A First of all, please check and see how many times a day he's eating. Often, children skip breakfast and eat only two meals a day. Their snacks are often junk food (potato chips, candy, etc.). I would advise your child to eat five to six times a day—and you must make sure that he eats breakfast, even if that means getting up a half hour earlier. The extra calories from the increased meals, combined with a weight training program (see Chapter Ten: Weight Training and the Young Athlete) will allow your son to build muscle mass and gain weight in a safe way.

Q Can an adolescent eat too much protein? If she consumes massive amounts of protein can something bad happen? What is the appropriate amount of protein for a young person?

A A young athlete should consume 50 to 80 grams of protein per day, based on her body weight. A portion of chicken or steak has about 25 grams of protein. But generally speaking, one cannot ingest too much protein. There are young athletes who may safely consume three steaks or eight slices of pizza at one time.

However, if a young athlete tries to boost his protein intake by taking protein shakes and amino acid supplements, there is a limit to how much the body can absorb. These substances are almost exclusively protein-based and contain very little carbohydrates or fat. Taken in excess, these products may cause abdominal pain and diarrhea because the body can't handle such a high protein load. In rare cases, kidney problems may result.

CHAPTER FIFTEEN

NUTRITIONAL SUPPLEMENTS AND STEROIDS

About three years ago, a sixteen-year-old boy named Ethan traveled from suburban Connecticut to see me at my New York City office. His complaint was back pain. Although I gave him a complete physical, including an X ray of the spine, he appeared to be perfectly healthy. After I attempted to give him an exercise routine, he said, "What I really came here for was antidepressants."

"I'm coming down off of steroids, and I need something," he suddenly shouted, adding, "I spend forty dollars a week on creatine, andro, ripped fuel, and protein shakes." I became wary of his mood changes, and the diagnosis was apparent. Aggressive behavior and erratic mood changes are severe side effects of steroid use, and withdrawal can make these adverse reactions even worse.

It is important to distinguish between nutritional supplements and performance-enhancing supplements. Nutritional supplements are generally considered vitamins, amino acids, and herbs. Performance-enhancing substances are purported to increase performance by improving muscle strength, quickness, and power. Both the supplements and performance-enhancing products are being marketed

toward youngsters. They are advertised in health and fitness magazines, on the Internet, and on the radio.

PERFORMANCE ENHANCERS

Muscle Strength Products

- *Steroids*. Anabolic steroids such as testosterone are substances that build muscle and strength and may allow the
muscles to be more explosive in their movements. They are
illegal and require a prescription. Steroids are normally used
to treat hormone deficiency and some types of cancer. But
when taken without regulation to "bulk up," they can be
especially dangerous.

   Steroids can produce mood swings, aggression, heart and
liver problems, premature closure of growth plates, acne,
unexplained fractures of the hips, and testicular atrophy.
Steroids can be taken orally or by injectable forms (intra-
muscular or intravenous). Products that are injected can
cause infections (HIV and more commonly hepatitis).

   We do know the short- and long-term consequences of
these products. Just ask the East German women athletes
who are suing their government for giving them steroids;
they were told they were vitamin pills—they are now infer-
tile and exhibit bouts of depression.

- *Human growth hormone*. This substance is a naturally occur-
ring hormone in the body. It helps stimulate overall growth,
especially in a growing child. It is available by prescription
only and is used in children who have low levels of the hormone, either from a tumor or from some other state of deficiency. It is, however, being used by professional and
Olympic athletes to build muscle strength. There are no documented reports of its use in children.

- *Creatine*. This substance is produced naturally in the body
and is found in meats. Athletes take it because they believe

it helps to improve muscle strength and power. It also is purported to allow athletes to work out harder and more intensely without fatigue. Creatine will not make a superstar out of a person who is normally a fair to average athlete.

My colleagues and I recently performed a study on sixth to twelfth graders regarding the usage of creatine. Our findings were: (1) Creatine is being used in children as young as the sixth grade. (2) There was a 5.6 percent overall usage rate. (3) Females were using creatine and in nonstrength sports (cheerleading, field hockey, and even gymnastics). (4) Twenty-five percent of students said they had a friend who was taking creatine.

The known side effects of creatine are dehydration and muscle cramps. Even mild dehydration can cause painful muscle cramps, and cases of severe dehydration can cause kidney failure and even death.

- *Andro.* Andro is short for androstenedione, which is metabolized in the body and becomes testosterone. It is banned by NFL football and NCAA, yet children have easy access to the product. It is purported to increase strength. One study in adults using Andro showed an increase in testosterone level as well as estrogen (the female hormone). Andro's short- or long-term effects have not been studied extensively in adults, and there are no studies done specifically for children regarding side effects or frequency of use. We do know that the short- and long-term side effects of testosterone can be devastating. We do not know how much andro is converted into testosterone and therefore do not know what a safe dose is.

WEIGHT GAIN PRODUCTS

There are a myriad of weight gain products, available under the names weight gainer fuel, amino acids, and protein shakes. One such product is labeled "Ripped Fuel," thereby giving a simple visual to its effects.

These products are often "safe," but still are responsible for frequent cases of diarrhea and abdominal pain.

A less expensive, and effective way to gain weight is to get more calories from a normal diet, along with a strength and conditioning program.

One example of a popular weight gain product:

- *Protein shakes.* Protein shakes that include amino acids (the building blocks of protein) are being used with increasing frequency. The powders that are sold to make up these shakes are a much more expensive way to receive the same protein that people consume in their normal diet—the advantage being that these shakes have a higher concentration of calories from protein.

  These products often do not contain adequate vitamins and minerals. Regular use of these drinks is known to produce varying degrees of abdominal pain and diarrhea. They could be used in addition to regular food and not as a substitute for a meal. The main concern is that the protein elements in the shakes are not as well absorbed as protein found in food products. In very high doses they can cause kidney problems.

WEIGHT LOSS PRODUCTS

If a young athlete wants to lose a few pounds, he might be tempted to try some of the newer weight loss products.

- *Herbal supplements.* The newest public approach to quick and easy weight loss are herbal products available through health food stores and the Internet. Herbs, such as chickweed, ginseng, kelp, and bee pollen, are often part of weight loss product mixtures, yet they actually do nothing to promote weight loss. The herb ephedra (ma huang) is sold as a product that can speed up metabolism. However, ephedra can cause dizziness, jitters, insomnia, and in rare cases strokes, heart attacks, and seizures.

- *Laxatives*. Laxatives are sold over the counter in drug stores and supermarkets. They are used to treat constipation and to promote bowel movements, but laxatives can also cause electrolyte (blood chemistry) imbalances. Athletes trying to lose weight—wrestlers, dancers, gymnasts—often use them. Distance runners who think that losing weight will make them run faster might also take laxatives.

- *Diuretics*. Diuretics are available only by prescription and are used to treat high blood pressure. Some athletes will resort to taking diuretics in an attempt to lose weight. Children or adolescents may get hold of these products from grandparents or other relatives. They can cause electrolyte imbalances, heart arrhythmias, dehydration, and dizziness.

Energy Boosters

- *Caffeine*. Children need to be warned about drinking too many caffeinated products—soda, coffee products, and tea. Caffeine, in high doses, is a banned substance in the Olympic programs. If six cups or more are consumed by an athlete, it may improve their running time in a sprint race. It is also an artificial stimulant, one which boosts heart rate and blood pressure in an active child, and is known to cause dehydration.

- *Ephedrine*. These drugs are often used as energy boosters or for weight loss. They often have terrible consequences such as arrhythmias, palpitations, and even death! They are not usually labeled as ephedrine, but if you read the label on products such as on No-Doz, you will recognize some by products of amphetamines. Ephedra is an herbal supplement used to aid weight loss because it speeds up the metabolism. I witnessed a football player faint on a hot September day after taking ephedra. Other over-the-counter products, such as many diet pills, weight loss products, or metabolism enhancers, contain varying quantities of ephedrine.

Nutritional Supplements

- *Energy bars.* These products contain various proportions of protein, carbohydrates, and fats; they may or may not be fortified with vitamins and minerals. These products can provide energy over an extended period of time when food products are not available. The advantage of these bars is that they are easy on the stomach. Above all, they are meant to be used as snack food, and not to replace a meal.

Supplement Safety: Tips for Parents

- Starting at a young age, initiate a discussion with your young athlete about proper diet, exercise, and nutritional supplements and performance-enhancing products.
- Find out exactly what is in any product your child is thinking about taking.
- Learn about any performance-enhancing drugs that other kids on the team are taking.
- Discuss and optimize proper nutrition and conditioning with your child.

Everyone who considers using nutritional supplements needs to weed out the fiction from the fact. Does anyone really know how safe these products really are? No one knows for sure, as long-term studies are not complete and short-term assessments by researchers need further evidence to shore up any conclusions.

The United States Food and Drug Administration (FDA), which checks out the safety of ingestible and absorbed products as well as pharmaceuticals before they are allowed to enter the competitive market, does not check the safety of these nutritional supplements. In 1993, the Proxmire Act was passed in Congress, which freed the FDA from overseeing the safety of nutritional supplements. In essence, this act has allowed the supplement industry to grow, without oversight from any federal agency. My advice for the consumer is to beware.

Another fact that athletes and their parents must understand is that many of the products have other chemicals added into the formulation. Creatine, for example, is produced in large quantities by many different manufacturers (just visit your local vitamin store). Each manufacturer may add other ingredients to the supplement and not label them.

Finally one must consider the purity of the product and quality control. When one buys acetaminophen or an antibiotic such as penicillin you know exactly what you are getting. You know that company A's product is as pure and potent as Company B's. With these "nutritional and performance-enhancing substances," one pill in the package may be more potent than another pill. In addition one company's product is usually not the same as the competitor's in terms of purity and consistency.

Learn as much as you can about these products before you let your child use any of them, and above all, have your child checked by your doctor before he takes any dietary supplements, including vitamins and minerals. If your child starts any supplement, watch out for warning signals such as abdominal discomfort, pain of any sort, rash, dizziness, or a lack of energy. If your child experiences any unusual side effects, then use of the product should be stopped immediately. Remember that no supplement can replace a healthy diet and a proper strength and conditioning program. There is no such thing as a "quick fix." If the results look too easy to obtain, they probably are.

If your child is contemplating the use of a nutritional or performance-enhancing product, consider the following:

- Is the product safe?
- Does it work?
- What can be done to bolster the same results using nutrition and exercise?

- What is the ideal dose?
- What special precautions need to be taken?
- What are the side effects?

Q&A WITH DR. SMALL

Q My fifteen-year-old son's friend from his football team has encouraged the team to use creatine and other nutritional supplements. He insists that these products are harmless and says that the fact that they are sold in health food stores should be indication enough of their beneficial effects. I know that these products are unregulated, and I have bad feelings about this. What do you think?

A I don't recommend using creatine or other performance-enhancing products for the very reasons you stated above. But if your son does use creatine, then make sure he takes it as recommended by the manufacturer. Be sure your son drinks plenty of liquids with this supplement to prevent cramping.

Q My seventeen-year-old daughter Andrea is a talented basketball player. In fact, she is in the running for a full athletic scholarship to college next year. Andrea says that her teammates are taking what they call "boosters" to get them psyched up before the game. What are boosters and should she be taking them?

A Your daughter's teammates are probably taking metabolites related to ephedrine, or "uppers." These products cause increase in heart rate and blood pressure. They can provide a rush of energy. They may also cause heart arrhythmias and even death.

The team members should be able to "psyche themselves up" for the game without any supplements. These products are banned in colleges and can lead to a loss of a college scholarship if someone tests positive.

Q My seventeen-year-old son is an all-state lacrosse player. He is 5 feet 11 inches tall and weighs 160 pounds. His high school coach and college coaches are telling him that he needs to gain twenty-five pounds in order to make a Division I college team. He is contemplating taking anabolic steroids. What do you think?

A I strongly recommend against taking the steroids. Although they work in the short-term (by building muscle and weight), they may have severe long-lasting adverse consequences, including liver damage, kidney damage, and mood swings. Instead, I would focus on building muscles by increasing calories in the diet, by eating five or six meals per day, and by taking part in a weight training program. (See Chapter Ten: Weight Training and the Young Athlete.) By the way, steroids are illegal unless given for a medical reason.

Q Everyone seems to be taking nutritional and performance-enhancing products. What are the alternatives?

A It is really not known what percentage of young athletes are taking nutritional supplements and performance-enhancing substances. I do not support the use of these products. The best way to improve one's performance in a sport is through hard work, practice, and good supportive coaching. To build strength, one needs to increase calories from protein and work out at least two to three times per week. To improve quickness and agility, the young athlete should practice various jumping and other plyometric drills.

Q Is there a relationship between using performance-enhancing substances and using alcohol and cigarettes? Will youngsters progress from performance-enhancing substances to taking recreational drugs or other hard drugs?

A There are no studies or information that discuss a relationship between using performance-enhancing substances and other illegal substances. One could make the argument that because of the pressure to succeed in today's society, especially in sports, these young-sters would be tempted to take steroids, human growth hormone, and even blood transfusions to win that national competition or college scholarship.

Q What do you think about taking vitamins?

A Vitamins are perfectly safe. In fact, I think most adolescents should be taking a multivitamin. However, they should not be taking superphysiological amounts—more than 300 percent of the Recommended Daily Allowance (RDA). This could result in toxici-ties. I do recommend that athletes eat fruits and vegetables that are high in Vitamins A, C, and E. These vitamins are antioxidants and can help in muscle recovery and heal injured tissue.

Q I found some pills in my son's backpack. I think they are steroids. What should I do?

A I would definitely confront your youngster about the pills—it's important to find out if they are steroids. I would not do this in an accusatory manner, however. Even if your son says "a friend gave it to him," and insists that he himself has not taken them, as a parent, I would suggest that you do further investigative work. I would try to find out if there is a teacher, coach, or student who is selling these products.

CHAPTER SIXTEEN

SPORTS PSYCHOLOGY

Marion, a twelve-year-old girl, plays basketball year-round. She plays in three different leagues and also travels to tournaments two to three times per month, often many hours away from home. As a result of all this activity, Marion's knees, ankles, and muscles are always bothering her. She is constantly fatigued. She became short-tempered, and her performance in games has recently declined. Her mother is afraid she has an illness.

Marion is suffering—not from an illness—but from overtraining syndrome, most commonly called burnout. Marion and her family need to realize this syndrome is caused by too much physical stress, which then leads to emotional distress. She doesn't have to quit basketball, but cutting back will help her gain perspective and allow her body to rest.

WHAT IS SPORTS PSYCHOLOGY?

The field of sports psychology is used to help kids develop skills to understand thoughts and feelings that interfere with optimal performance and enjoyment of their sport. This often requires the use of a professional sports psychologist, although many times commonsense changes in a kid's schedule are all that's needed. Sports psychology in kids is most commonly used for serious athletes, not casual players who are actively involved in and committed to their sport.

The various problems that sports psychology can help are:

- Over-training syndrome, commonly called burnout
- "Choking" under pressure, or an inability to perform at a sporting event
- Performance enhancement: how to concentrate during competition, how to be in the zone, and how to deal with anxieties that affect performance
- Resolution of interpersonal conflicts: between the athlete, parent, coach, or team players
- Feeling overwhelmed, dealing with life's issues and pressures, and how to prioritize and organize
- Dealing with pressure during competition
- Quitting: making decisions about when to retire from the competitive world
- Recovering from injury: how to deal with the physical and emotional aftereffects

We'll examine each problem in turn, and discuss how work with a sports psychologist will help your young athlete overcome her difficulty.

BURNOUT/OVER-TRAINING SYNDROME

The majority of kids who are involved in sports actually enjoy them. But often, kids see a sport as too much of a time commitment, or they feel too much pressure, causing them to feel unhappy or conflicted about whether to continue. Knowing what's considered "normal" behavior for your child can help you recognize even small changes in his actions, which may be an early warning that something is wrong. The behaviors to watch for include a decrease in athletic performance, talking about quitting sports, withdrawal from friends, decline in grades, or avoidance of clubs the child had actively participated in previously. Also look out for changing sleep patterns, eating problems, evasiveness, irritability, lying, apathy, sadness, or physical complaints.

Solutions for Burnout

The solution to athletic burnout requires a bit of creativity. There are three scenarios that usually help those who have over-trained and are burnt out: (1) taking a break and stop training altogether for two to six weeks, (2) continuing to compete but cutting back training by 50 percent and keeping practice time "fun," and (3) eliminating competition and practicing only for fun, gradually getting back into the competitive spirit three to nine months later.

CHOKING

There are children who play extremely well in practice, but who "choke" in competition. They strike out with the bases loaded, double fault in tennis on match or set point, or miss a wide-open goal in hockey or soccer. Finding a solution to "choking" is not always simple because it requires finding the precise cause of the problem. There may be many reasons for choking such as:

- Fear of losing, or not living up to expectations
- Fear of winning or succeeding
- Inability to control thoughts, instead of concentrating on the task at hand
- Not having enough experience

Solutions for "Choking"

Fear of winning or losing involves confidence issues, but it can be rooted in complex thoughts and emotions that need to be identified and then addressed. A fear of winning can stem from the athlete's lack of experience and a confusion of how to react to the situation at hand. For example, if an athlete is thinking about what to say to her team-mates and coach after she wins, she won't be able to fully focus on the game as it's being played. Conversely, an athlete may be so terrified of losing that it preoccupies him during play and prevents him from doing his best. A helpful hint for young athletes is to convince them to stay in the moment—to concentrate on one object, such as the pitcher's hand or the opponent's racquet. With only one thing to "look" at, the athlete's mind will clear.

Lack of concentration will cause lack of focus on the task at hand. Often when a young athlete sees the opportunity to score a goal, sink the winning basket, or make a difficult shot, she "rushes," becoming overly anxious and making an error. One solution is to count to three, take a deep breath and try to do things in slow motion. Some athletes do not know what to focus on and must be taught; others need relax-ation training.

Not having enough experience may be improved upon as familiarity with the competitive situations improves. Practice sessions that simu-late competitive game situations maybe helpful; although nothing can replace the real competition experience.

PERFORMANCE ENHANCEMENT

Sometimes an athlete does well on the field but doesn't perform up to his personal best. As we discussed earlier, a lack of concentration may get in the way of young athletes performing their best. They may lack focus. They might be thinking of a boyfriend or girlfriend, homework, or maybe going to the mall. Or they may be having distracting thoughts—about having to win, what people will think of them, about previous failures. There are many tools that can help the young com-petitor. These include: visual imagery, auditory stimuli, breathing techniques, relaxation training, and deliberate training on what to focus on in the particular sport.

Techniques for Performance Enhancement

Visual imagery can sharpen concentration skills. An athlete can imagine the baseball pitcher's hand, the quarterback's throwing arm, or an opponent's tennis racquet. This technique helps to prevent the mind from drifting off. Young athletes can use mental imagery to picture hitting a home run, catching the football to win the game, or serving an ace down the middle of the court.

Auditory stimuli can help the athlete to focus in on relevant sounds to initiate concentration. Perhaps the sound whistle, the blast of a gun before the start of a track meet, or the whirring sound of skate blades on ice will stimulate your young athlete's senses and focus attention.

Breathing techniques aid athletes by helping them to relax before a competition so they are ready to compete.

Relaxation training may take the form of self-hypnosis or biofeedback—learning to contract and relax one's muscles as well as control one's blood pressure or heart rate. Other techniques involve learning to focus on specific sensations or external stimuli to aid concentration.

INTERPERSONAL CONFLICT

An inevitable part of growing up is experiencing conflict with other people, especially parents. These family conflicts may concern curfew, going out with friends, homework, dating, and time management. The result of this interference may be an inability to focus on training and competition.

Although a sports psychologist may be needed to resolve these issues, parental guidance might do the trick. Talk to your child; find out what he is feeling. If your child can be helped to unwind and sort through his mental anxiety, he can focus and enhance his game. If your child absolutely won't talk to you, it may be time to call upon a specialist in this area. A specialist can screen your child for larger, more serious issues, such as depression or suicidal thoughts. If your child becomes combative or emotionally withdrawn, medical attention should be sought immediately.

FEELING OVERWHELMED

Many young athletes feel overwhelmed, on and off the court, with responsibilities. Your youngster may feel the burden of a team sport, feel pressure to score, or feel the need to perform a certain way on the field. During the season, it might seem as if there is not enough time for all their activities, such as homework, family responsibilities, friendships, and other sports.

Regarding the pressure to succeed, kids need to be reminded that even professional athletes have this problem. As maturity and self-confidence grows, your child will hopefully respond better to pressure. One helpful idea is to make a schedule that makes room for all of her activities. This can be a flexible schedule (daily, weekly, and monthly), but it helps the athlete to feel organized and less overwhelmed. Keep in mind, this schedule is a work in progress, and can be changed and modified any time. Elite athletes may need to have parents and/or coaches meet with school personnel to discuss an individual and flexible academic plan.

PRESSURE DURING COMPETITION

There is not a competitor alive who does not sometimes get nervous or feel "butterflies" in the stomach before an important competition. This is part of human nature. It often is helpful to establish a pregame ritual—such as eating and drinking, listening to music, and stretching and warming up with exercises before the game. Being physically occupied helps the athlete to relax and become better focused. During the competition, athletes can try to concentrate on one visual, auditory, or physical cue.

QUITTING

Why is it that, according to the National Association of Sports and Physical Education, almost 75 percent of boys and girls quit organized sports by the time they are twelve years old? Some athletes find the responsibility and time commitment involved with sports too difficult. This is particularly true of older elite child athletes. There are several specific reasons for the fallout and some possible solutions as to how parents and coaches can keep children involved in physical activity, without pressuring them.

Kids cite many reasons for quitting sports, including:

- The activity ceases to be fun
- The sport becomes too competitive
- They don't like to compete against their friends
- The sport is too much of a time commitment
- Sports make them unable to focus on other interests or goals

Whatever the reason that your child chooses to quit, it's important to talk about the decision together. Gently urge your child to tell you why she is making this decision. This could be quite difficult, because your child may not be conscious of the real reason. You might try asking specific questions, such as:

- Is there something involving team activities, a specific person, or even the coach that bothers you?
- Are you sure that quitting is the right choice?
- Is there anything that could be changed that would make you want to stay involved?

RECOVERING FROM INJURY

There is not a competitive athlete around who hasn't experienced some type of injury—be it major or minor. It is the major injury, or season-ending one, that may cause physical or emotional damage to the young athlete. Once the young athlete has "recovered" from his injury and has been cleared to return to competition, there are often uncertainties in the athlete's mind. The athlete may wonder:

- Will he be as good as he was before?
- Will he get injured again?
- Is he fragile or weak in some way that caused him to be injured in the first place?

The solutions to these uncertainties lies with the mental strength and self-confidence of the athlete. The young athlete in this instance may be assisted by a parent, a coach, or a sports psychologist to overcome his injury and move forward in competition. The young athlete must set realistic expectations regarding his performance after the return to competition. An adequate time period to recover physical skills is critical.

Q & A WITH DR. SMALL

How do I find a sports psychologist in my community?

This is a frequently asked question. You can contact the U.S. Olympic Training Center in Colorado Springs, Colorado, for a reference. Also contact the national governing body of the particular sport that your child plays, such as American Youth Soccer Association (AYSO), USA swimming, United States Tennis Association, etc. You can contact the American Psychological Association; they have a subgroup listing for sports psychology. Finally, you can contact your local hospital or medical school and speak with someone in the Department of Psychology or Psychiatry for a reference. When you call the recommended professional, ask him how many child athletes he has worked with successfully.

Q *What background and training should a sports psychologist have?*

A The sport psychologist does not necessarily have to be an actual psychologist. This person might be a social worker or a coach who has a strong background in sports therapy. It is best if the professional has a clinical background working with kids. It would be great if this individual played competitive sports so she can best understand your youngster and what it means to be in competition.

Q *I have a twelve-year-old son. He is on three soccer teams (a school team, a town team, and a travel team). I think that this is too much. What can I say to get him to cut back?*

A Three soccer teams at the same time do seem like a lot. However, it is possible that he is able to handle it. Ask yourself the following questions: Is he doing well in school? Does he seem to have a lot of energy? Is he in good spirits? Is he usually in good health without injury or pain? If your son is enjoying his active routine and the answers to these questions are all "yes," let him continue.

Q *My seventeen-year-old son has not been pitching well this past season. How do I know if it is a psychological problem, or if it is a mechanical one?*

A This is not a simple question to answer. You should never simply assume that a problem is a psychological issue. Your son may have changed his pitching mechanics inadvertently. There may be an injury—acute or chronic—that is leading to his decreased performance, or a virus, such as mono, might be a factor as well. If all of these possibilities don't pan out, then you could pursue the sports psychology route. This is not a simple question to answer, and you may want to involve your son's pediatrician in solving the problem.

Q My *twelve-year-old daughter seems to be "burnt out" from figure skating. It has been recommended that she see a sports psychologist. She refuses because she says she's not crazy and the sports psychologist will not be able to help her. What do I tell her?*

A I usually explain to youngsters that sports psychologists don't generally work with the mentally ill. I would tell your daughter that the psychologist helps many young athletes improve their performance. You should try to convince your daughter to go at least once to see how it goes. After that, let her choose if she wants to continue.

Q *My son is a physically gifted athlete. He likes contact sports— hockey, football, and lacrosse. In competition, however, he does not play up to potential and is not aggressive enough. Can a sports psychologist help?*

A If you choose to seek out the advice of a professional, then a sports psychologist can help. This person, together with your son, can explore the reasons for his suboptimal game performance. He may be fearful of getting injured or severely injuring another player. Or, his mind may just be drifting off during competition. Whatever the reason, the psychologist may help to identify the problem and help focus his mind during game time.

Q *If I choose to seek the help of a professional to help my daughter focus better during competition, does it have to be only a professional sports psychologist?*

A Child athletes deal with the same life issues common to all kids. Often, these concerns will be reflected in their physical performance, even though the issues are not related. Bearing this in mind, consider what the real concerns of your child are. A child psychologist might be all you need.

Q My son gets very nervous before a big game. Should I seek out a professional sports psychologist, or should I deal with his nerves on my own?

A You can certainly try to help your son on your own and see how it goes. Go to your library or bookstore to look for books on sports psychology. They will offer you good tips on how to best handle your son's nerves. If this is not helpful to your son, then seek out the advice of a professional to help tackle the problem.

CHAPTER SEVENTEEN

THE SPORTS PARENT

*My children enjoy playing soccer, and at each game one parent
is responsible for bringing snacks and drinks. On one particular
day it was very hot and humid; I brought an extra water bottle
for my son, just in case there was not enough water, or if my son
did not like the drink selection. My son was six at the time, and
in our town his age group practiced for half an hour and played
a game for half an hour. During practice time, my son would run
over and take a drink. Again, it was very, very hot. The coach
got very angry and insisted my son only take a drink with the
team. After twenty minutes of practice, the team still had not
taken a drink.*

*All athletes, especially the young ones, must keep hydrated
while participating in sports. Thinking more about my child than
about the team, I insisted my son have his water. I was more
concerned with being a good parent.*

It is tough being a good parent. There are many decisions that you
must make everyday to ensure the best for your children and your family. If your kids are involved in sports, there are even more decisions
to make in order to help your child to become fit, happy, and active.
Common sense is your best tool. This chapter is divided into various
segments, to help you with questions on being the best sport parent
possible.

ENCOURAGEMENT

Encourage your child, and you will give him the confidence to succeed. Confident children will do better in sports. They will try harder, concentrate better, and will put more effort into learning the game. Encouragement also includes helping your child to practice, ensuring she has the right equipment, showing up at games, and watching her inline skate, skateboard, or whatever sport or physical activities she likes to do.

If you push your child too much or do not give enough encouragement, your child will not feel confident. Children will often give up on a sport they do not feel secure in. Recently, I had a family in my practice with two boys, ages eight and ten. The younger boy was a gifted athlete, and the older boy was slightly above average. The parents kept focusing on the eight-year-old and ignored the ten-year-old. I told the parents, in a private setting, that the ten-year-old needed encouragement for sports as well.

NUTRITION

Whatever sport or physical activity your child is playing, it is important that she have adequate nutrition and hydration so the muscles, body, and brain are fueled and prepared for activity. You should review Chapter Fourteen: Nutritional Guidance for the Active Child, but as a brief overview, children should drink eight ounces of water beyond their thirst level before a game or exercise. They should drink another four to eight ounces of water every fifteen to thirty minutes while exercising. Snacks should be healthy and not loaded with fat. Kids should snack every two to three hours to keep their energy level up.

A child who has a game or practice at 10 A.M. on a weekend morning without having breakfast will most likely fatigue early, not perform to her best, and is at greater risk for injury. Similarly, a child who has a game at 3 P.M. on a school day and has not eaten anything since 10:30 A.M. will be starving and will not be able to concentrate on his athletic event.

INJURY MANAGEMENT

It is likely that at some time your child will get injured playing sports. It might be an insignificant scrape, but an injury could also be serious enough to seek medical attention. It is up to you as a sports parent to determine the difference between a minor or major injury. It is also important for parents to take your kids in for a second opinion if necessary.

Here are some helpful tips for when to take your child to the doctor:

Subtle Signs

- If your child complains of a joint pain or muscle ache for more than two weeks.
- If your child suffers from a slight limp on several occasions at the end of a game.
- If there is a decrease in performance (for example, used to run three miles in twenty-one minutes and is now running it in twenty-five minutes).
- If there is a personality change (used to be very outgoing and is now antisocial).

Obvious Signs

- Unable to bear weight on a limb
- Swelling of a joint
- Deformity of a limb
- Loss of consciousness at an athletic event
- Persistent headaches, dizziness, and nausea even after minor head trauma

TRAINING

If your child enjoys a sport, take the time to help her improve skills. You will boost your child's confidence and increase her enjoyment. There are a myriad of opportunities to advance the sport skills of your child—private lessons, sports camps, or of course, practice time with parents, siblings, or teammates.

Here are the particulars:

- Always make practices and games fun.
- Look for training programs that teach skills or are character building, and are not just about winning or losing.
- Vary the training with cross-training techniques. Weight training or plyometrics (a training technique using various jumping exercises to improve power, quickness, and jumping ability) are good ways to start.

FAN RAGE

Recently in Staten Island, New York, a father punched his son's hockey coach because the son didn't play the last two minutes of the game. This father took the game much too seriously.

In Florida, a mother roughed up a seventeen-year-old referee who managed her son's soccer team because she didn't like his call.

In another highly publicized incident in Massachusetts, one hockey father did not like the way the coach was conducting practice. After the practice, the father and the coach were involved in a fight, which resulted in the coach's death. Children at the rink witnessed the entire episode.

It's not unusual for parents' emotions to run high and low during the course of their child's game. Good sports parents must remain calm and in control. If you are getting too emotional, take a break, walk away, and compose yourself.

INAPPROPRIATE BEHAVIOR BY ADULTS IN STANDS

There are times when parents get so involved in a child's sporting event that they say or do inappropriate things. I still remember a baseball game when I was eleven; an adult from the opposing team was yelling at me when I was pitching: "You're no good; You'll walk everyone around the bases; You don't know how to pitch." He was obviously trying to rattle me and disrupt my concentration. Although I didn't give up baseball, my confidence was temporarily shaken.

TEACHING SPORTSMANSHIP

I try to tell my children, my patients, and the kids I coach to cheer, encourage, and applaud teammates, and never to taunt or yell at opponents. Sports offer the unique opportunity to teach children how to work with others, how to deal with losing and adversity, how to learn from mistakes, and how to improve one's performance.

One way to teach sportsmanship and goodwill is to have a discussion after the child's game. I find this effective with my own children. I discuss two topics. First, we discuss their performance. For example, after a soccer game, we might discuss whether they scored any goals, whether they saved any goals, or whether they made any good passes. Second, we discuss sportsmanship and behavioral issues. It is traditional to line up and shake hands with the other team after the conclusion of a game. One time our team won, and my son said, "Ha-ha, we won, you lost." Now, this is natural for a seven-year-old, but I spent some time that evening explaining that his comments were not productive and most likely hurt many of the other players' feelings.

Many children do not wish to discuss a losing game right away. Discussions about their behavior on the playing field might have to wait until they are able to talk about it. Some kids are more likely to talk to a coach than to a parent.

GIVE YOUR CHILD THE REWARD OF REST

One of the most important factors to touch upon is the issue of sleep. Your child needs adequate sleep to perform all the responsibilities of a day. Without proper rest, you may notice your kid "sagging" in the middle of the day. Children under the age of ten need eight to ten hours of sleep a night. Children over the age of ten need seven to nine hours a night.

In addition to adequate sleep, parents should ensure that their kid is getting the right amount of rest between practices and competitions. A child should not practice or train in the same sport seven days a week. It is best to train only four to five days a week.

If your child is an elite athlete, it is your job as parent to set your son or daughter's training plan. It's important that every three or four months, there is a period of one to two weeks of rest from their chosen sport. This point is especially critical, as rest allows muscles to recover from hard work and the mind to relax, reducing the possibility of burnout.

This is what a good sports parent should do:

- Look for a coach who gives positive messages.
- Be a model for other parents, coaches, and the kids. If you feel the urge to yell, take a walk to cool down.
- Reassure your child that making a mistake is normal and is part of the experience. All athletes make mistakes, even Olympians.
- Emphasize effort over result. Do not blame your child when there is a loss.
- Be reasonable in the presence of those who display irrational behavior.
- Remember that your coach is often a volunteer and is donating her time to your child. A coach needs your respect.
- Do not blame the kids whose parents drive you crazy!

Q&A WITH DR. SMALL

Q My son is six years old and involved in soccer. My complaint is that there seems to be no real organization at all in the practice. From your opinion, how should a good practice session be run?

A Here is how a coach should arrange a team practice for kids aged six to nine:

- The practice from start to finish should not be longer than ninety minutes.
- The first five or ten minutes should be used as a warm-up period, including aerobic activity such as jumping jacks, running around the field, running in place, or a combination of the above.
- Next comes five to ten minutes of stretching. The coach will perform the stretches and make sure that all the children are doing them correctly.
- The coach will then move on to five to ten minutes of drills, involving passing, shooting, and dribbling. These skills will be incorporated into the game itself.
- The last set of practice will be two-on-one or three-on-two drills, which involve passing and shooting on the goal.
- Healthy snacks and drinks should be provided for the team members.
- Games should last no longer than forty-five minutes, and the teams should be arranged by splitting the practice squads into equal teams.
- Following the game, the coach should again have the kids stretch and perform cooldown exercises.
- And last, but certainly not least, the coach and volunteers should boost egos by praising team spirit and action.

Q When is a child playing or practicing too much, and when do I as a concerned parent request the coach to lighten up?

A If your child has too many injuries, has an injury that doesn't heal in a timely fashion, feels burnt-out, has a personality change, has become short-tempered, or feels overly tired then he is probably playing too much. If your child has demonstrated several of these traits, then he may be suffering from overtraining syndrome. (See Chapter Sixteen: Sports Psychology.)

Some coaches are always looking for new training techniques. This can be great, but the coach also has to be responsive to each child's needs and health concerns. In one case I saw, a coach told a young athlete she needed to improve her explosiveness and suggested jumping rope. She took his advice and began jumping rope every day on her hard concrete driveway. After two weeks, this youngster ended up with a stress fracture in her lower shin from doing too much jumping on a hard surface.

It is your role as sports parent to critically appraise training techniques. If you feel your child is in danger of being injured, then you must step in, even if the situation is uncomfortable.

Q *What do I do if a coach is verbally abusive to my child?*

A Unfortunately, this situation seems to be on the rise, and there is no straightforward answer. You could try arranging a meeting with the coach to discuss your issues. You may want to ask other parents on the team if their children have been affected as well. You should definitely try speaking with the coach first. If you witness no change in behavior and no resolution of the problem, a talk with league officials would be appropriate. Some people might opt for removing the child from the team.

Q *What should I do if the parents of kids on the team are abusive and demonstrate poor conduct toward opposing team members?*

A There are a number of approaches to this situation:

- You should privately try to speak with the coach about this. The coach may or may not be aware of what is going on. You can brainstorm together and come up with some suggestions.
- You can take your child off the team.
- You can create a committee or interest group that focuses on sportsmanship and behavioral issues.

Q *Can I allow my eleven-year-old child to travel across the country alone with her coach?*

A I would highly recommend, if at all possible, traveling with the coach and your child. Your coach may be very qualified and great with kids, but there have been many instances of child abuse and molestation. If accompanying your child is not possible, I would advise another parent or relative to go with them as a chaperone.

Q *My son is fourteen, a freshman in high school, and is going out for varsity football. It is tradition that all of the freshmen shave their heads before their first scrimmage. He feels silly and alienated and does not want to. What should I do?*

A This is hazing—an initiation right common in youth sports across the United States. Wearing funny clothes or shaving heads are relatively benign acts. Whether to participate is up to your son—if there's no bullying or coercion involved, I would probably recommend that your son shave his head. He would probably be the subject of a great deal of teasing if he does not do so. However, if there were more violent or intrusive acts such as paddling on parts of body, I would recommend that he not participate in that hazing act. In addition, if there are violent hazing activities the coach or athletic director should be notified.

Q *My daughter has a cough and a cold. Can she play in tonight's basketball game?*

With just a cold (upper respiratory infection), she can play in tonight's game. If she has a fever, she must wait to have a normal temperature for at least twenty-four hours before participation. If one does vigorous exercise with fever, there is the possibility of myocarditits, an infection in the heart.

My son is fourteen and is going to Europe with his soccer team for one week this summer. Is there anything he should do to prepare for the trip?

On the plane ride over, he should avoid caffeinated beverages and try to drink four to eight ounces of fluid every hour to keep himself hydrated. If possible, the team should not play a game or a match for at least three or four days. The children would need to get acclimated to the time difference, as well as the food (it would be ideal if the team brought all or some of their meals from the United States).

In professional sports today, one sees pitchers throwing bats and football players throwing their helmets in disgust. Are there any role models left in today's professional sports? Should I let my children watch sports on television?

Unfortunately, television and the rest of media often focus on the negative. There are plenty of positive stories. Not watching sports on television is not the solution. However, it probably takes more effort today to discuss the negative actions and displays of behavior that we see on television.

My daughter is twelve and a high-level gymnast. She's also a straight A student and trains twenty hours per week. She is at the gym from 6–9 P.M. and doesn't eat dinner until 9:30 P.M. She then has two to three hours of homework each night. She gets up at 6 A.M. She's tired and dragging herself around. Do you have any suggestions?

A First off, you should make sure she's getting enough to eat. You should pack your daughter at least two drinks and a healthy snack or a small meal (yogurt and fruit, or a half a sandwich and a piece of fruit) to eat while at gymnastics. Also it would be wise to make more efficient use of her time for doing her homework. She could do thirty minutes to one hour when she gets home from school, and thirty minutes while at gymnastics. Your daughter can also eat part of her dinner on the car ride home. She's probably not getting enough sleep. She should get at least eight hours per night and more on the weekend.

Conclusion

As we all know, it is not easy being a good, responsible parent. There are many schedules to deal with, family and school issues to worry about, religious activities to attend, as well as after school activities; the list goes on and on.

The good news is that we can include sports and physical activity within all this daily activity. It's fun, it's good for all of us, and it helps make our day and our child's day that much better. If your child is physically fit, or is on the way towards improving his physical health, your child will behave better, do better in school, probably stay off drugs, and most important, feel better about himself.

You must consider proper training techniques so your kids don't hurt themselves. If an injury does occur, you must know when to take them to the doctor and how to manage the injury, which often includes rehabilitation. And of course, no matter what, nutrition is always important, which includes eating properly before, during, and after competition, as well as throughout the year.

Regarding the elite athlete, don't expect stardom or excellence right away. It takes years of training for your child to reach such a high level of distinction. In order to achieve excellence in a sport, the child athlete needs the support of a sports medicine team, including parents, coaches, and physicians.

Regardless of your child's health and medical condition (being overweight, or suffering from asthma, diabetes, or neuromuscular disability) she can reap the benefits of being physically active: improved strength, heart and lung fitness, and improved self-esteem.

Finally, in order to ensure your child's enjoyment of sports, optimize his athletic performance, and assist him in choosing appropriate sports, one needs to know the appropriate questions to ask your doctor and other experts.

1) If your child is injured, you should ask the following questions:

- How long will it take for function to return?
- What types of rehab exercises are needed?
- How long will it take to return to practicing the sport?
- How long will it take to return to full sports participation?

2) If your child needs surgery, you should ask the following questions:

- Are there alternatives to surgery?
- How many surgeries has the surgeon done in the past year? How many has she done in her total career?
- Are you comfortable with the hospital she will have the surgery in?
- If the surgery is complicated have you sought a second opinion?

3) If your child wants to specialize in one sport year-round, you should ask the following questions:

- Does your child love the sport?
- Does your child have a good coach?

- Does your child have a good working relationship with a personal physician and other health care professionals (nutritionist, physical therapist, sports psychologist)?

4) If your child is contemplating a weight-training program:

- Does your child have a qualified adult instructing?
- Is your child focusing on form and technique rather than the amount of weight lifted?
- Is your child focusing on high repetitions and low weights?

5) If your child is contemplating taking nutritional supplements:

- Is your child optimizing a nutrition and conditioning program?
- Does your child know the short- and long-term side effects of the product?
- Does your child have any known medical conditions (problems with heat stroke, kidney problems, or heart arrhythmias)?

Keep in mind: You are a role model. It is important to set an example by keeping fit yourself. If you are physically active, it is more likely that your children will be active. Then, everyone is a winner on this road towards good health. So get your kids moving, and have fun!

Resources for Parents

CHAPTER ONE

Bly, L. *Motor Skills Acquisition in the First Year*. New York: Academic Press, 1994.

Clements, R.L. and M. Lee. *Parent's Guide to Physical Play*. New York: American Association for the Child's Right to Play, 1998.

Council for Physical Education for Children. *Physical Activity for Children: A Statement of Guidelines*. Reston, VA: National Association for Sport and Physical Education, 1998.

Green, M. and J. S. Palfrey, eds. *Bright Futures: Guidelines for Health Supervision of Infants, Children, and Adolescents* (2nd ed.). Arlington, VA: National Center for Education in Maternal and Child Health, 2000.

Eliot, L. *What's Going On in There? How the Brain and Mind Develop in the First Five Years of Life*. New York: Bantam Books, 1999.

Fox, S. *Baby Steps: Exercises for Baby's First Year of Life*. New York: Berkley Publishing Group, 1999.

Meltzoff, A. N., A. M. Gopnik, and P. K. Kuhl. *The Scientist in the Crib: Minds, Brains and How Children Learn*. New York: Morrow/Avon, 1999.

National Association for Sport and Physical Education. *Active Start: A Statement of Physical Activity Guidelines for Children Birth to Five Years*. Reston, VA: National Association for Sport and Physical Education, 2002.

CHAPTER TWO

Katzman, C. S., R. McCary, and D. Kidushim-Allen. *Helping Your Child Be Healthy and Fit: With Activities for Children Aged 4 through 11*. Washington, DC: Office of Educational Research and Improvement, U.S. Department of Education, 1993.

Landy, J. and K. Burridge. *50 Simple Things You Can Do to Raise a Child Who Is Physically Fit*. New York: Macmillan, 1997.

Shisler, J., R. Killingsworth, and T. Schmid. *Kidswalk-to-School: A Guide for Community Action to Promote Children Walking to School*. Atlanta: Centers for Disease Control and Prevention, National Center for Chronic Disease Prevention and Health Promotion, 1999.

CHAPTER THREE

Kalish, S. *Your Child's Fitness: Practical Advice for Parents*. Champaign, IL: Human Kinetics Publishers, 1996.

CHAPTER FOUR

Wolff, R. *Good Sports: The Concerned Parent's Guide to Competitive Youth Sports*. New York: Sports Publishing, Aug. 1998

CHAPTER FIVE

Silby, C. and S. Smith. *Games Girls Play: Understanding and Guiding Young Female Athletes*. New York: St. Martin's Press, Aug 2000.

Women's Sports Foundation. *Sports Injury Concerns: The Female Athlete*. East Meadow, NY: Women's Sports Foundation, 1992.

Women's Sports Foundation. *Sports in the Lives of Urban Girls: A Resource Manual for Girls' Sports in Urban Areas*. East Meadow, NY: Women's Sports Foundation, 1999.

CHAPTER SEVEN

Cassel, D. K. *The Encyclopedia of Obesity and Eating Disorders*. New York: Facts on File, 1994.

Jablow, M. M. *A Parent's Guide to Eating Disorders and Obesity*. New York: Bantam Doubleday Dell Publishing Group, 1992.

Clark, N. *Nancy Clark's Sports Nutrition Guidebook*, 2nd ed. Champaign, IL: Human Kinetics, 1996.

Ikeda, J. P. *If My Child Is Overweight, What Should I Do About It?* Oakland, CA: University of California, Division of Agriculture and National Resources, 1998.

Levine, J. *Helping Your Child Lose Weight the Healthy Way*. Secaucas, NJ: Birch Lane Press, 1996.

Jablow, M. M. *A Parent's Guide to Eating Disorders and Obesity*. New York: Bantam Doubleday Dell, 1992.

Kosharek, S. M. *If Your Child Is Overweight: A Guide for Parents*. Chicago: The American Dietetic Association, 1993.

CHAPTER EIGHT

Allen, L., ed. *Physical Activity Ideas for Action: Secondary Level*. Champaign, IL: Human Kinetics, 1997.

Allen, L., ed. *Physical Activity Ideas for Action: Elementary Level*. Champaign, IL: Human Kinetics, 1997.

Sammann P. *Active Youth: Ideas for Implementing Physical Activity Promotion Guidelines*. Human Kinetics Publishers, 1998.

CHAPTER NINE

Capper, L. *That's My Child: Strategies for Parents of Children with Disabilities*. Washington, DC: Child and Family Press, 1996.

Goldberg, B., ed. *Sports and Exercise for Children with Chronic Health Conditions*. Champaign, IL: Human Kinetics, 1995.

Greenstein, D., N. Miner, E. Kudela, and S. Bloom. *Backyards and Butterflies: Ways to Include Children with Disabilities in Outdoor Activities*. Brookline, MA: Brookline Village Books, 1997.

Betschart, J. and L. M. Siminerio. *The Guide to Raising a Child with Diabetes*, 2nd ed. Alexandria, VA: American Diabetes Association, 1999.

Wysocki, T. *The Ten Keys to Helping Your Child Grow Up with Diabetes*. Alexandria, VA: American Diabetes Association, 1997.

CHAPTER TEN

Fleck, S. and W. Kraemer. *Designing Resistance Training Programs*. Champaign, IL: Human Kinetics, 1997.

Kraemer, W. and S. Fleck. *Strength Training for Young Athletes*. Champaign, IL: Human Kinetics, 1992.

CHAPTER ELEVEN

Griffith, H. *Complete Guide to Sports Injuries: How to Treat Fractures, Bruises, Sprains, Strains, Dislocations, Head Injuries*. New York: Putnam Publishing Group, 1986

Micheli, L. *The Sports Medicine Bible: Prevent, Detect, and Treat Your Sports Injuries Through the Latest Medical Techniques*. New York: HarperCollins, 1995.

CHAPTER TWELVE

Shamus, E. and J. Shamus. *Sport Injury Prevention and Rehabilitation*. New York: McGraw-Hill, 2001.

CHAPTER THIRTEEN

Chu, D. *Plyometric Exercises with the Medicine Ball*. Bittersweet Publishing, 1989.

CHAPTER FOURTEEN

Clark, Nancy. *Nancy Clark's Sports Nutrition Guidebook*. Champaign, IL: Human Kinetics, 1996.

Dietz, W. H., and L. Stern, eds. *Guide to Your Child's Nutrition: Making Peace at the Table and Building Healthy Eating Habits for Life*. Elk Grove Village, IL: American Academy of Pediatrics, 1999.

Jennings, D. S. and S. N. Steen. *Play Hard, Eat Right: A Parents' Guide to Sports Nutrition for Children*. Minneapolis, MN: Chronimed Publishing, 1995.

Tamborlane, W., J. Z. Weiswasser, N. A. Held, and T. Fung. *The Yale Guide to Children's Nutrition*. New Haven, CT: Yale University Press, 1997.

CHAPTER FIFTEEN

Headley, S. and Susan J. Massad. *Nutritional Supplements for Athletes*. Reston, VA: American Alliance for Health Physical, 1998.

CHAPTER SIXTEEN

Murphy, S. *The Cheers and Tears: A Healthy Alternative to the Dark Side of Youth Sports Today*. New York: Jossey-Bass Inc., March 1999.

Murphy, S. *Sports Psychology Interventions*. Champaign, IL: Human Kinetics, Jan 1995.

CHAPTER SEVENTEEN

Wolff, R. *Coaching Kids for Dummies*. Foster City, CA: IDG Books Worldwide, 2000.

Wolff, R. *Good Sports: The Concerned Parent's Guide to Competitive Sports*. New York: Dell, 1992.

OTHER RESOURCES

American Academy of Family Physicians
11400 Tomahawk Creek Parkway
Leawood, KS 66211-2672
1-800-274-2237
(913) 906-6000

American Academy of Pediatrics
141 NW Point Boulevard
Elk Grove Village, IL 60007-0927
(847) 228-5005
www.aap.org

American Academy of Podiatric Sports Medicine
4414 Ives Street
Rockville, MD 20854

American College Health Association
P.O. Box 28937
Baltimore, MD 21240-8937
(410) 849-1500
www.acha.org

American College of Sports Medicine
401 West Michigan Street
Indianapolis, IN 46206-1140
(313) 637-9200
www.acsm.org

American Diabetic Association
1701 North Beauregard Street
Alexandria, VA 22311
1-800-342-2383
www.diabetes.org

American Lung Association
1740 Broadway
New York, NY 10019
(212) 315-8700
www.lungusa.org

American Medical Society for Sports Medicine
11639 Earnshaw
Overland Park, KS 66210
(913) 327-1415

American Orthopaedic Society for Sports Medicine
6300 North River Road, Suite 200
Rosemont, IL 60018
(847) 292-4900
www.sportsmed.org

American Physical Therapy Association
Sports Physical Therapy Section
N3227 State Road 16, Suite D
LaCrosse, WI 54601

American Running Association/American Medical Athletic Association
4405 East West Highway, Suite 405
Bethesda, MD 20814
(301) 913-9517
www.americanrunning.org

American Society of Testing & Materials
100 Barr Harbor Drive
West Conshohocken, PA 19428-2959
(610) 832-9710

American Youth Soccer Organization
National Support and Training Center
12501 S. Isis Avenue
Hawthorne, CA 90250
1-800-872-2976
www.soccer.org

Canadian Academy of Sports Medicine
1010 Rue Polytek Street
Unit 14, Suite 100
Gloucester, ON Canada K1J9H9
(613) 748-5851
www.casm-ACMS.org

Centers Disease Control & Prevention
4770 Buford Highway NE, MS K-46
Atlanta, GA 30341-3717
(770) 488-5692

The Center for Sports Parenting
The Feinstein Building
3045 Kingstown Road
Kingston, RI 02881
www.sportsparenting.org

Easter Seals
230 West Monroe Street, Suite 1800
Chicago, IL 60606
1-800-221-6827
www.easter-seals.org

Little League Baseball
P.O. Box 3485
Williamsport, PA 17701
(570) 326-1921
www.littleleague.org

March of Dimes
1275 Mamaroneck Avenue
White Plains, NY 10605
1-888-663-4637
www.modimes.org

National Association of Children's Hospitals and Related Institutions
401 Wythe Street
Alexandria, VA 22314
(703) 684-1355
www.childrenshospitals.net

National Association of Collegiate Directors of Athletics
P.O. Box 16428
Cleveland, OH 44116
(216) 892-4000

National Association of Intercollegiate Athletics
6120 South Yale Avenue, Suite 1450
Tulsa, OK 74136
(914) 494-8828
www.naia.org

National Association for Sports & Physical Education
1900 Association Drive
Reston, VA 20191
(703) 476-3410

National Athletic Trainers Association
2952 Stemmons Freeway, Suite 200
Dallas, TX 75247
(214) 637-6282
www.nata.org

National Collegiate Athletic Association
P.O. Box 6222
Indianapolis, IN 46206-6222
(317) 917-6222
www.ncaa.org

National Federation of State High School Associations
P.O. Box 90
Indianapolis, IN 46206
(317) 972-6900
www.nfhs.org

National Strength and Conditioning Association
1955 North Union Blvd.
Colorado Springs, CO 80909
(719) 632-6722

National Youth Sports Safety Foundation Inc.
333 Longwood Avenue, Suite 202
Boston, MA 02115
www.nyssf.org

North American Society for Pediatric Exercise Medicine
1607 North Market Street
P.O. Box 5076
Champaign, IL 61825
1-800-747-4457
(217) 351-2674

Pony Baseball and Softball
International Headquarters
P.O. Box 225
Washington, PA 15301
www.pony.org

Sport Information Resource Center
116 Rue Alberta Street, Suite 400
Ottawa, Ontario, Canada
K1P 5G3
(613) 231-7472
www.sportsquest.com
www.sportdiscus.com

United States Figure Skating Association
20 First Street
Colorado Springs, CO 80906
www.usfsa.org

United States Olympic Committee/Sports Medicine Committee
One Olympic Plaza
Colorado Springs, CO 80909
(719) 578-4546

United States Tennis Association
70 West Red Oak Lane
White Plains, NY 10604-3602
1-800-990-8782
http://national.usta.com

USA Gymnastics
Pan America Plaza
201 South Capitol Avenue, Suite 300
Indianapolis, IN 46225
(317) 237-5050
www.usa-gymnastics.org

Bibliography

Arendt E., Dick R. "Knee Injury Patterns Among Men and Women in Collegiate Basketball and Soccer." NCAA data and review of literature. *American Journal of Sports Medicine* 23, No. 6 (Nov-Dec 1995): 694-701.

Bar-Or, O. et al. "Physical Activity, Genetic, and Nutritional Considerations in Childhood Weight Management." *Medicine and Science in Sports and Exercise* 30, No. 1 (Jan. 1998): 2-10.

Bar-Or, O. *Pediatric Sports Medicine for The Practitioner. From Physiologic Principles to Clinical Applications.* New York: Springer, 1983.

Barrett, J., Kuhlman, G., Stanitski, C., and Small E. "The Preparticipation Physical Evaluation" in *Care of the Young Athlete,* edited by Sullivan, J.A. and Anderson, S.J. American Academy of Orthopaedic Surgeons and American Academy of Pediatrics, 2000.

Committee on Public Education, American Academy of Pediatrics. "Children, Adolescents, and Television." *Pediatrics* 107, No. 2 (Feb. 2001): 423-426.

Committee on Sports Medicine and Fitness, American Academy of Pediatrics. "Climatic Heat Stress and the Exercising Child and Adolescent." *Pediatrics* 106, No. 1 (July 2000): 158-159.

——. "Intensive Training and Sports Specialization in Young Athletes." *Pediatrics* 106, No. 1 (July 2000): 154-157.

——. "Medical Concerns in the Female Athlete." *Pediatrics* 106, No. 3 (Sept. 2000): 610-613.

——. "Medical Conditions Affecting Sports Participation." *Pediatrics* 107, No. 5 (May 2001): 1205-1209.

——. "Risk of Injury from Baseball and Softball in Children." *Pediatrics* 107, No. 4 (April 2001): 782-784.

——. "Strength Training by Children and Adolescents." *Pediatrics* 107, No. 6 (June 2001): 1470-1472.

Committee on Sports Medicine and Fitness, American Academy of Pediatrics. "Organized Sports for Children and Preadolescents." *Pediatrics* 107, No. 6 (June 2001): 1459-1462.

——. "Physical Fitness and Activity in Schools." Pediatrics 105, No. 5 (May 2000): 1156-1157.

Committee on Sports Medicine and Fitness, American Academy of Pediatrics. "Physical Fitness and Activity in Schools." *Pediatrics* 105, No 4 (April 2000): 868-870.

Dehaven, K.E., Linter, D.M. "Athletic Injuries: Comparison by Age, Sport, and Gender." *American Journal of Sports Medicine* 14 (1986): 218-224.

Delo, M., Small, E. "Athletic Injuries in Youth: A Two-Year Retrospective Review at a Hospital Sports Clinic." *Office and Emergency Pediatrics* 12 (1999): 192-197.

Metzl, J.D., Small, E., Levine, S.R., and Gershel, J.C. "Creatine Use Among Young Athletes." *Pediatrics* 108, No. 2 (Aug. 2001): 421-25.

Micheli, L.J. "Overuse Injuries in Children's Sports: The Growth Factor." *Orthopedic Clinics of North America* 14, No. 2 (Apr 1983): 337-360.

Otis, C.L., Drinkwater B., Johnson M., Loucks A., and Wilmore J. American College of Sports Medicine Position Stand. "The Female Athlete Triad." *Medicine and Science in Sports and Exercise* 25, No. 5 (May 1997): i-ix.

Rowland, T. *Exercise and Children's Health.* Champaign, IL: Human Kinetics, 1990.

Rowland, T. (ed.) *Pediatric Laboratory Exercise Testing: Clinical Guidelines.* Champaign, IL: Human Kinetics, 1993.

Ruud, J. *Nutrition and The Female Athlete.* Boca Raton, FL: CRC Press, 1996.

Small, E. *The Preparticipation Sports Physical in Primary Care of Adolescent Girls.* Edited by Coupey S.M. Philadelphia: Hanley and Belfus Publisher, 2000.

——. "Knee Pain in the Pediatric Patient." *Office and Emergency Pediatrics* 2001; 14(1): 31-34.

Small, E. and Bar-Or, O. "The Young Athlete with Chronic Disease." *Clinical Journal of Sports Medicine* 14, 3 (July 1995).

Smith, A.D., Tao, S.S. "Knee Injuries in Young Athletes." *Clinical Journal of Sports Medicine* 14 (1995): 629-650.

Stanitski, C.L. "Pediatric and Adolescent Sports Injuries." *Clinical Journal of Sports Medicine* 16 (1997): 613-633.

Yeager, K.K., Agostini R., Nattiv, A., Drinkwater, B. "The Female Athlete Triad: Disordered Eating, Amenorrhea, Osteoporosis." *Medicine and Science in Sports and Exercise* 25, No. 7 (July 1993): 775-7.

Index

ERIC SMALL, M.D., F.A.A.P., is a nationally recognized expert in pediatric/adolescent sports medicine, and is one of only a handful of physicians in the United States with this concentrated specialty. He frequently appears on radio and television as a featured expert, and works with ranked tennis players, top gymnasts, elite figure skaters, and national soccer players.

He is Clinical Assistant Professor of Pediatrics, Orthopedics, and Rehabilitation Medicine at Mount Sinai School of Medicine in New York, and is Director of the Sports Medicine Center for Young Athletes at Blythedale Children's Hospital in Valhalla, New York. Dr. Small serves on the American Academy of Pediatrics Committee on Sports Medicine and Fitness and serves as a medical consultant to Girl Scouts of America and The Center for Sports Parenting. As a pediatric sports medicine specialist, he takes care of young athletes who have suffered from a sports injury or want to participate in sports after an injury.

Dr. Small performed his pediatric residency at Albert Einstein College of Medicine/Montefiore Medical Center in New York, a fellowship in pediatric exercise medicine at McMaster University in Hamilton, Ontario, Canada, and a Pediatric Sports Medicine Fellowship at Boston Children's Hospital-Harvard Medical School in Boston. Dr. Small is founder and former Chairperson of the United States Tennis Association/Eastern Section Sports Science Committee.

A life-long athlete, he played high school baseball and was a star varsity tennis player at Haverford College. He has coached children since he was fifteen years old. In addition, he has taught and coached his own four young sons. He resides with his wife and sons in Westchester County, New York.

LINDA SPEAR has been a frequent contributor to *The New York Times* for nineteen years, and is the author of *The Downsized Woman: A Survival Guide*. Previously, Spear was the host of a weekly talk show "Let's Talk Health" for a Westchester-based radio station (WFAS/AM). In addition, she served as Manager of Corporate communications for Ciba-Geigy Corporation in Tarrytown, New York, and as Manager of Public Relations at Phelps Memorial Hospital Center in Sleepy Hollow, New York. Currently, Ms. Spear develops and implements communications initiatives for companies as diverse as Bayer Diagnostics, Reader's Digest Association, and the Family Service Society of Yonkers. Spear earned a Bachelor of Science degree from Temple University and a Masters of Science from the University of Pennsylvania. She lives in Dobbs Ferry, New York.